PARTICIPANT'S GUIDE

Other Resources by Lee Strobel

The Case for Christ
The Case for Christ audio
The Case for Christ — Student Edition (with Jane Vogel)
The Case for Christ Study Bible
The Case for a Creator
The Case for a Creator audio
The Case for a Creator — Student Edition (with Jane Vogel)
The Case for Easter
The Case for Faith
The Case for Faith audio
The Case for Faith — Student Edition (with Jane Vogel)
The Case for the Real Jesus
The Case for the Real Jesus — Student Edition (with Jane Vogel)
Experiencing the Passion of Jesus (with Garry Poole)
God's Outrageous Claims
Surviving a Spiritual Mismatch in Marriage (with Leslie Strobel)
Surviving a Spiritual Mismatch in Marriage audio

Other Resources by Garry Poole

The Complete Book of Questions
Seeker Small Groups
The Three Habits of Highly Contagious Christians

In the Tough Questions Series:

Don't All Religions Lead to God?
How Could God Allow Suffering and Evil?
How Does Anyone Know God Exists?
Why Become a Christian?
Tough Questions Leader's Guide (with Judson Poling)

PARTICIPANT'S GUIDE

EXPLORING
CHRISTIANITY'S
TEN
TOUGHEST
QUESTIONS

LEE **STROBEL** AND
GARRY **POOLE**

ZONDERVAN

ZONDERVAN.com/
AUTHORTRACKER
follow your favorite authors

We want to hear from you. Please send your comments about this book to us in care of zreview@zondervan.com. Thank you.

ZONDERVAN

Faith Under Fire Participant's Guide

Tough Faith Questions Participant's Guide
Copyright © 2006 by Lee Strobel and Rocket Pictures

Faith and Facts Participant's Guide
Copyright © 2006 by Lee Strobel and Rocket Pictures

Faith and Jesus Participant's Guide
Copyright © 2006 by Lee Strobel and Rocket Pictures

This title is also available as a Zondervan ebook. Visit www.zondervan.com/ebooks.

Requests for information should be addressed to:

Zondervan, *Grand Rapids, Michigan 49530*

ISBN 978-0-310-68786-3

Cover design: Micah Kandros
Interior design: Sherri L. Hoffman

Printed in the United States of America

12 13 14 15 16 17 /DCI/ 22 21 20 19 18 17 16 15 14 13 12 11 10 9 8 7 6 5 4 3 2 1

CONTENTS

Preface   7

session 1   Is the Supernatural Real?   9

session 2   Is Jesus a Prophet or the Son of God?   19

session 3   Did Jesus Rise from the Dead?   33

session 4   Do All Roads Lead to God?   45

session 5   Is the Bible Bogus?   61

session 6   Does Science Point toward a Creator?   75

session 7   Is Anything Beyond Forgiveness?   91

session 8   Why Does God Allow Pain and Suffering?   103

session 9   The Mystery of the Trinity?   117

session 10   Do Christians and Muslims Worship
             the Same God?   133

Special thanks to Ann Kroeker and Laura Allen
for their outstanding writing and editing contributions.
Their creative insights and suggestions took
this guide to the next level.

PREFACE

The idea came to me in the shower one morning: why not create a television program in which people of various beliefs—from Muslims to Christians to atheists to New Agers—could debate the most provocative spiritual and moral issues of the day?

What's more, prominent religious leaders could be invited on the program to be cross-examined about the stickiest questions concerning their faith.

Thanks to the vision and creativity of Jim Berger and Joni Holder, we ended up producing *Faith Under Fire*™ for a national television network. As predicted, the weekly show generated a slew of vociferous letters from viewers around the country. More than one person admitted that he found himself shouting back at his TV set.

This curriculum is based on the interviews and debates we aired on the program. You'll see knowledgeable and passionate experts discussing not just *what* they believe, but *why* they believe it. Our hope is that your group will provide a safe environment for you to be able to share your own thoughts and opinions—as well as to consider the viewpoints of others.

You'll quickly see that many of the claims made by the experts are mutually exclusive. In other words, the Christian and Muslim cannot both be right if the Bible claims Jesus is the Son of God and the Koran asserts that he's not divine but merely a prophet. One of them might be correct, or both of them could be in error, but each one of them cannot be true at the same time.

That's why we insist that our experts back up their claims. Can they defend their position logically? Do they have evidence from history or science that supports their assertions? Our task should be to determine where the evidence points.

In a similar way, the U.S. Constitution provides equal protection to all expressions of faith, and yet that doesn't mean all religious claims are equally true. According to the U.S. Supreme Court, the American ideal is to create a "marketplace of ideas" in which various opinions and beliefs can freely battle with each other so that truth will ultimately prevail.

So what is "true" about God, about Jesus, and about the afterlife? What can we know with confidence about issues of faith and morality? I hope you'll grapple with these issues in unhindered debate and discussion in your group.

One thing is true for sure: a lot hinges on the outcome.

Lee Strobel

IS THE SUPERNATURAL REAL?

Read It!

Wishful Thinking?

As spotlights streak across the world-famous monument, suspense spreads among the live audience of New Yorkers gathered to witness the spectacle. With the dramatic flair of a seasoned showman, David Copperfield shocks and amazes an estimated fifty million people watching by television—the Statue of Liberty *disappears*! Go figure. Is it a miracle, magic, or a trick of the eye?

Intricate patterns and complex geometric designs mysteriously appear in farm fields overnight. Aerial photographs offer the best view of these veritable works of art created by flattened wheat and corn crops: people around the world are calling them *crop circles*. Are they alien navigational tools, electromagnetic natural occurrences, or a group of talented artists tromping around at midnight with boards strapped to their feet?

A twenty-year-old Estonian woman lost her sight after a head injury when she was a little girl. Doctors diagnosed lifelong disability. During a televised 2003 healing conference, however, she put her hands on her eyes during a service and prayed along with the leader. "When I took my hands away I was able to see!" she exclaimed. Miracle, magic, or a staged television scam?

An Arizona housewife's psychic ability to communicate with the dead helps solve crimes, piecing together complicated, confusing clues. Is it an accurate source for legitimate investigations, supernatural communication from God, satanic activity, or simply an intriguing concept for a prime-time television show?

Moses stretched out his hand over the Red Sea, and all night long a strong east wind drove the waters back and formed a path of dry land. With a wall of water on their right and left, the Israelites crossed over to the other side without getting wet—not even a single drop. Miracle, myth, a great scene for a bearded Charlton Heston, or a natural occurrence with lucky timing?

When Jesus fed a crowd of five thousand with only five loaves of bread and two fish, he looked up to heaven, gave thanks, and handed the meager food to the disciples, who in turn passed it to all the people. Everyone ate and was satisfied, and when they counted the leftovers, there were twelve basketfuls. Did the food miraculously multiply, did the disciples make it all up, or did Jesus simply inspire the crowd to pull out their hidden lunches and share what was already there?

Do miracles really happen? Or are they the exaggerated result of mere wishful thinking? This is a foundational issue to the identity of Jesus of Nazareth. To believe he's the unique Son of God who proved it by rising from the dead, we need to first believe the supernatural is possible. But is it—*really*?

Watch It!

Use the following space to take notes as you view the video in which Lee Strobel interviews Dr. J. P. Moreland, a Christian philosopher, and skeptical attorney Edward Tabash.

Discuss It!

1 Consider the following list of events: a spectacular sunset, the birth of a baby, the healing of a broken bone, a complete recovery from cancer without medical treatment, and a man walking on water. Which of these events, if any, would you label as a miracle? Why?

2 Define *miracle*. Define *supernatural occurrence*. Is a miracle a supernatural occurrence and vice-versa? Explain.

3 Have you or anyone you know ever had a personal experience that you believe to be a modern-day miracle or a supernatural occurrence? Tell about that experience.

4 Why do you suppose many people find it difficult, if not impossible, to believe in miracles? What about you? Do you think it is logical and reasonable to believe a supernatural realm exists? Why or why not?

> "There are two ways to look at life. One is that nothing is a miracle, and the other is that everything is a miracle."
>
> **Albert Einstein**

5 J. P. Moreland outlines three strands of evidence to support the occurrence of the supernatural: "Bangs have bangers, rigged dice have riggers, and information (referring to DNA) has informers." How well do you believe these three categories of evidence support belief in the supernatural? Why?

6 Edward Tabash argues that "if there really is a banger, a dice thrower, and an informer, then such a being should not play dice with our knowledge and should be more amenable to direct experience. But we have no evidence of the types of miracles that allegedly occurred in the Bible happening today." Do you agree or disagree with Tabash's argument that if some kind of divine being—God—is real, then there should be more sufficient evidence of the occurrences of modern-day miracles? Explain your answer.

7 Dr. Moreland claims that healings occur today. Do you agree with his statement? Why or why not?

8 To what extent do you think miracles are a product of exaggerated hope or delusional thinking? To what extent do you think miracles are genuine? Explain.

9 Dr. Moreland suggests that the mere existence of human free will is strong evidence of a realm beyond the natural realm of cause and effect. Does this line of reasoning make sense to you? Why or why not?

"For nothing can happen without cause; nothing happens that cannot happen, and when what was capable of happening has happened, it may not be interpreted as a miracle. Consequently, there are no miracles.... We therefore draw this conclusion: what was capable of happening is not a miracle."

Cicero, *De Divinatione*, 2.28

10 The Oxford American Dictionary defines the word *supernatural* as: "Of, or caused by, power above the forces of nature"; and the word *miracle* as: "A remarkable and welcome event that seems impossible to explain by means of the known laws of nature and is therefore attributable to a supernatural agency." Assuming that supernatural events such as miracles *do* occur—even rarely—would you say that by definition, *any occurrence* of the miraculous must necessitate the existence of some kind of divine being? Why or why not?

"A miracle ... is an event that cannot be given a natural explanation but must be attributed directly to God, who has acted in a special way in the natural order."

C. Stephen Evans, *Why Believe?*

11 Explain why you agree or disagree with the following statement: "If God doesn't exist, by definition miracles don't happen, because a miracle is an act of God. If, on the other hand, God does exist and he is the creator of the universe, miracles are possible because the God who created everything has the power to choose to do something else."

12 Consider the purpose of miracles. John 2:23 says, "Now while he [Jesus] was in Jerusalem at the Passover Feast, many people saw the [miraculous] signs he was doing and believed in his name." John 10:24–25 says, "The Jews who were there gathered around him [Jesus], saying, 'How long will you keep us in suspense? If you are the Messiah, tell us plainly.' Jesus answered, 'I did tell you, but you do not believe. The works [miracles] I do in my Father's name testify about me.' " According to these passages, what is the value of miracles? Even though we are twenty centuries removed from the events, how is this point still valid?

"First, whatever begins to exist has a cause. Second, the universe began to exist. And, third, therefore, the universe has a cause. As the eminent scientist Sir Arthur Eddington wrote: 'The beginning seems to present insuperable difficulties unless we agree to look on it as frankly supernatural.' "
Theologian William Lane Craig

Watch It! Lee's Perspective

There was a time when I would have agreed wholeheartedly with Edward Tabash: the supernatural is a figment of wishful thinking. As an atheist, I ruled out the possibility of a supernatural realm. Later, though, I became more open-minded. I decided to follow the evidence of science and history wherever it pointed—even if it seemed to indicate that miracles are possible and that the supernatural exists. Based on the kind of scientific evidence that Dr. Moreland describes, as well as the convincing historical evidence for the resurrection of Jesus that I describe in my book *The Case for Christ*, I became firmly convinced that the universe is the product of a Creator and that Jesus of Nazareth is truly his Son. To me, that's the most logical conclusion I could reach. So here's my question for you: does it make more sense to deny the supernatural because of an assumption that it's impossible, or to follow the evidence wherever it leads?

Chart It!

At this point in your spiritual journey, what do you believe about miracles? On a 1–10 scale, place an X near the spot and phrase that best describes you. Share your selection with the rest of the group and give reasons for placing your X where you did.

1	2	3	4	5	6	7	8	9	10

I'm not convinced miracles occur.　　　I'm unsure what to believe about miracles.　　　I'm convinced miracles occur.

Study It!

Take some time later this week to check out what the Bible teaches about miracles and the supernatural.

• Jeremiah 32:17–21, 26–27
• Matthew 8:23–27
• John 11

IS JESUS
A PROPHET
OR THE
SON OF GOD?

Read It!

Human Disguise?

Mild-mannered Clark Kent stutters and stammers through a meeting with his editor at *The Daily Planet*. When Lois Lane enters the room, he frantically fumbles his notes and nervously takes a sip of coffee. As his thick glasses slowly slide down his nose, he shoves them back using the heel of his hand, but spills hot coffee down the front of his shirt.

Moments later, as Clark is blotting the coffee stain, a change comes over his face. His super hearing has detected the screams of men and women miles away—a train's brakes have failed, and sparks fly as its wheels screech against the tracks. Hundreds of passengers are trapped as the train travels faster and faster, out of control toward a broken bridge.

Our "weakling" friend makes up a quick excuse, rushes out of the office to a nearby phone booth, and emerges as someone his coworkers would never expect: Superman!

Leaping over Metropolis skyscrapers in a single bound, he flies at supersonic speed to rescue the runaway train as it hurtles toward disaster. Seconds before the train plunges into the abyss, Superman transports the train and all its passengers safely to the other side! He even goes back and repairs the damaged track. All is well again. Superman saves the day!

What a hero!

Too bad he doesn't exist. We sure could use someone like him to intervene in our world and make things right. But Superman is the stuff of comic books and film. Nobody believes in Superman.

Well, there *are* some who believe in a superman of sorts, only they call him by a different name: Jesus Christ.

Jesus wasn't a comic book creation; his story has been around a whole lot longer than Superman's. Jesus came to us as a baby born in a manger over two thousand years ago. He grew up and developed quite a following, with people traveling alongside him from town to town. He told stories and taught lessons. Some say he was a great teacher; others claim he was a prophet, speaking the words of God to all who would listen.

But Jesus Christ had a normal side. He ate food with his disciples, drank water, got hot and thirsty and tired. Impressive as he was, he still seems weak and needy—which sounds rather ordinary and human.

Then again, the records state he turned water into wine, made blind men see, and fed five thousand people with a little boy's lunch. And as the story goes, he appeared to heal people from various diseases and even bring people back from the dead. He didn't fly, but some say he walked on water. Later, after his death, they claim he came back to life and appeared to his family and a whole bunch of friends and followers. They even argue that soon afterward, he ascended into heaven.

That sounds a lot like some kind of a superman. Did Jesus have a secret identity? Was he hiding that he was more than a human? Was Jesus really God in human disguise?

Some think Jesus was much more than a teacher or a prophet. They believe Jesus was God himself, God in the flesh. If so, he had far more than superhuman powers. If Jesus was God, he was the perfect One intervening in a history that he himself created. Divine. All-powerful.

Yet unbelievable, the stuff of myths and comic books.

It would be nice, though, wouldn't it? It would be so nice to really have some kind of a superman living among us, listening for our cries for help, some kind of a hero to rescue us ... to save us.

Watch It!

Use the following space to take notes as you view the video in which Lee Strobel interviews Mike Licona, the founder of Risen Jesus, a Christian organization based in Virginia Beach, and Shabir Ally, the founder of the Islamic Information Center in Toronto, Canada.

Discuss It!

1 As a group, take a few moments to list some of the common words or phrases you have heard used to describe or define Jesus Christ.

2 When you were growing up, what were you taught about Jesus?

3 What do you believe about Jesus *today*? Is he a good man? A prophet? The Messiah? The divine Son of God? What words or phrases do you think accurately describe him? On what do you base your beliefs about Jesus?

> "Suppose, however, that God did give this law to the Jews, and did tell them that whenever a man preached a heresy, or proposed to worship any other God that they should kill him; and suppose that afterward this same God took upon himself flesh, and came to this very chosen people and taught a different religion, and that thereupon the Jews crucified him; I ask you, did he not reap exactly what he had sown? What right would this god have to complain of a crucifixion suffered in accordance with his own command?"
>
> **Robert Ingersoll,** *Ingersoll's Works,* **Vol. 2**

4 Shabir Ally considers Jesus to be a prophet born of a virgin, a miracle worker, and the Messiah who was raised from the dead. But he does not believe Jesus to be divine (or the "Son of God") in any way. Does Ally's conclusion make sense to you? Why or why not? Does his belief that Jesus is not divine contradict any of his other beliefs about Jesus? Explain.

5 Based on the following excerpts from the New Testament, who do you think Jesus believed himself to be? Give reasons from the text for your responses.

> The high priest said to him, "I charge you under oath by the living God: Tell us if you are the Messiah, the Son of God." "You have said so," Jesus replied. "But I say to all of you: From now on you will see the Son of Man sitting at the right hand of the Mighty One and coming on the clouds of heaven." (Matthew 26:63–64)

[Jesus] said, "Do you believe in the Son of Man?" "Who is he, sir?" the man asked. "Tell me so that I may believe in him." Jesus said, "You have now seen him; in fact, he is the one speaking with you." Then the man said, "Lord, I believe," and he worshiped him. (John 9:35–38)

Jesus answered, "I am the way and the truth and the life. No one comes to the Father except through me. If you really know me, you will know my Father as well. From now on, you do know him and have seen him." Philip said, "Lord, show us the Father and that will be enough for us." Jesus answered, "Don't you know me, Philip, even after I have been among you such a long time? Anyone who has seen me has seen the Father. How can you say, 'Show us the Father'?" (John 14:6–9)

[Jesus answered] "I and the Father are one.... Why then do you accuse me of blasphemy because I said 'I am God's Son'?" (John 10:30, 36b)

For just as the Father raises the dead and gives them life, even so the Son gives life to whom he is pleased to give it. Moreover, the Father judges no one, but has entrusted all judgment to the Son, that all may honor the Son just as they honor the Father. Whoever does not honor the Son does not honor the Father, who sent him. Very truly I tell you, whoever hears my word and believes him who sent me has eternal life and will not be judged but has crossed over from death to life. (John 5:21–24)

> "'Son of Man' is often thought to indicate the humanity of Jesus, just as the reflex expression 'Son of God' indicates his divinity. In fact, just the opposite is true. The Son of Man was a divine figure in the Old Testament book of Daniel who would come at the end of the world to judge mankind and rule forever. Thus, the claim to be the Son of Man would be in effect a claim to divinity."
>
> **William Lane Craig**

6 Both Mike Licona and Shabir Ally agree that the Gospels provide the earliest historical record of the life and ministry of Jesus Christ (written by eyewitnesses during the lifetimes of many other eyewitnesses). How reliable do you think the Gospels are as an historical source of information about the life and ministry of Jesus? Explain.

> "The Koran does not claim to be a better historical record. The Koran reaffirms earlier historical records, namely the Gospels themselves, and it calls upon people to judge by what God has revealed in the Gospels."
>
> **Shabir Ally**

7 Licona believes there is historical evidence that Jesus claimed divinity and rose from the dead. Ally suggests that Jesus' divinity is really an idea that simply evolved over time. Who do

you agree with most? Why? In what ways do the following *early* accounts from the Gospels impact what you believe about the true identity of Jesus?

> Then John [the Baptist] gave this testimony: ... I have seen and I testify that this is God's Chosen One." (John 1:32, 34)

> Immediately Jesus reached out his hand and caught him [Peter]. "You of little faith," he said, "why did you doubt?" And when they climbed into the boat, the wind died down. Then those who were in the boat worshiped him, saying, "Truly, you are the Son of God." (Matthew 14:31–33)

> Jesus said to her [Martha], "I am the resurrection and the life. The one who believes in me will live, even though they die; and whoever lives by believing in me will never die. Do you believe this? "Yes, Lord," she replied, "I believe that you are the Messiah, the Son of God, who is to come into the world." (John 11:25–27)

> Thomas said to him [Jesus], "My Lord and my God!" Then Jesus told him, "Because you have seen me, you have believed; blessed are those who have not seen and yet have believed." Jesus performed many other signs in the presence of his disciples, which are not recorded in this book. But these are written that you may believe that Jesus is the Messiah, the Son of God, and that by believing you may have life in his name. (John 20:28–31)

8 Licona argues that Jesus had two natures—a divine nature and a human nature. Conversely, Ally counters that "to be human means to have limitations and to be divine means to have no limitations. Jesus cannot be limited and unlimited at the same time unless he was schizophrenic." What do you think? Was Jesus schizophrenic? Why or why not? Is it possible or impossible for Jesus to be both completely human and completely divine at the same time? Could theologians be right when they say, based on Philippians 2, that during Jesus' earthly ministry he voluntarily emptied himself of the independent use of his divine attributes? Explain.

9 Read John 20:28–31 (see reference on page 27). What do you think it would take (or what did it take) for you to come to the same conclusion as Thomas and say—as he finally did— "[Jesus, you are] my Lord and my God!" (v. 28)?

10 What are some of the implications for all of humanity if Jesus really was the unique Son of God?

11 What are some implications for *your* life if Jesus really was God in human form? Which of these implications is most difficult or troublesome to you?

> "When Jesus came to the region of Caesarea Philippi, he asked his disciples, 'Who do people say the Son of Man is?' They replied, 'Some say John the Baptist; others say Elijah; and still others, Jeremiah or one of the prophets.' 'But what about you?' he asked. 'Who do you say I am?' Simon Peter answered, 'You are the Messiah, the Son of the living God.' Jesus replied, 'Blessed are you, Simon son of Jonah, for this was not revealed to you by flesh and blood, but by my Father in heaven.'"
>
> **Matthew 16:13–17**

Watch It! Lee's Perspective

As a skeptic, I once thought the Gospels were merely religious propaganda, hopelessly tainted by overactive imaginations and evangelistic zeal. However, my extensive investigation of the historical evidence convinced me that they reflect eyewitness testimony and bear the unmistakable earmarks of accuracy. So early are these biographies that they cannot be explained away as legendary invention. In fact, the fundamental beliefs in Jesus' miracles, resurrection, and especially his deity go way back to the very dawning of the Christian movement. Historian Gary Habermas has even found seven ancient secular sources and several early creeds concerning the deity of Jesus, a doctrine that he said is "definitely present in the earliest church." Going even further, New Testament scholar Ben Witherington III went back to the very earliest traditions, which are unquestionably safe from legendary development, and was able to show that Jesus had a supreme and transcendent understanding of himself. Based on the evidence, Witherington told me: "Did Jesus believe he was the Son of God, the anointed one of God? The answer is yes. Did he see himself as the Son of Man? The answer is yes. Did he see himself as the final Messiah? Yes, that's the way he viewed himself. Did he believe that anybody less than God could save the world? No, I don't believe he did."

Chart It!

At this point in your spiritual journey, who do *you* say that Jesus is? On a 1–10 scale, place an X near the spot and phrase that best describes you. Share your selection with the rest of the group and give reasons for placing your X where you did.

1	2	3	4	5	6	7	8	9	10

I'm very certain Jesus was an extraordinary man, but he was not God in human form.

I'm in a fog concerning who Jesus was.

I'm very certain Jesus was God in human form just as he claimed he was.

Study It!

Take some time later this week to check out what the Bible teaches about Jesus and his identity.

- Mark 2:1–12
- Luke 5:20–26
- Luke 22:66–71
- 1 John 2:23

DID JESUS RISE FROM THE DEAD?

Read It!

Really Risen?[1]

Powerful thunder cracks overhead like colossal whips. The earth seems possessed, quivering and then convulsing underfoot. Some unseen force slashes the temple curtain from top to bottom. A terrified guard shouts in awe, "Surely he was the Son of God!" For a time, darkness blankets the confusion, as if all are buried alive ...

... all except One. There is One who has breathed his last. For him, it is finished. It is finally finished. The pandemonium fades. The spectators disperse. The earth settles.

Stillness.

Silence.

Clean linen, a new tomb in a quiet garden, a huge stone. The Sabbath invites those who love him to wait, to rest. For Jesus, there is ultimate rest—from the pain, the suffering, the degradation. No more whips across the back or strikes into the face. No more beatings or bruises. The sentence has been carried out. The debt to society has been paid. It is done. It is over.

Or is it?

Early morning, the first day of the week, Mary Magdalene goes to the tomb with some other women. *But wait.* The stone is rolled back. The strips of linen are laid aside, the burial cloth folded neatly by itself. The tomb ... it's empty!

His body is gone—he's not there! Two men gleaming like lightning stand beside the trembling women. "Why do you look for the living among the dead? He is not here; he has risen!"

Risen?

They rush to the disciples to tell them the news. He's risen—he's alive!—just as he had foretold. Peter and John race to the tomb and find it just as the women had said: Empty. Jesus is gone!

Where is he?

---

1. Introduction written by Ann Kroeker. Used by permission.

Jesus shows up everywhere. He spends time with Mary, two others on the road to Emmaus, and then Peter and the disciples. After that, he even appears to a group of five hundred. He cooks breakfast for his friends. He talks. He eats some fish. He is very much alive. They still wonder, *Is it really true?*

"Why are you troubled, and why do doubts rise in your minds?" he asks them. "Look at my hands and my feet. It is I myself! Touch me and see; a ghost does not have flesh and bones, as you see I have." They still find it hard to believe despite their joy and amazement! *It can't be ... can it? Can he really and truly be alive?*

Yes, it's him! Without question, this is his body. The marks of the crucifixion are still evident: the nail-punctured hands and feet, the pierced side. How can he be alive after all that physical torment? How can he be walking around, talking with people, eating a broiled fish?

He patiently extends an invitation to Thomas, the doubter, "Put your finger here; see my hands. Reach out your hand and put it into my side. Stop doubting and believe."

Thomas does. The doubter touches, sees—and believes. "My Lord and my God!" Thomas exclaims, convinced that this is Jesus, the One he saw crucified, dead, and buried. And the One who rose again on the third day exactly like he said he would. Now here he is—healed, though scarred, and standing alive before them all.

So, the dead hero comes back to life. How about that—a storybook ending! Everyone's delighted! At least Jesus and his friends are. And that's that, right? All's well that ends well. Close the book and move on.

Right?

Watch It!

Use the following space to take notes as you view the video in which Lee Strobel interviews Dr. William Lane Craig, one of the world's leading authorities on the resurrection, and Richard Carrier, an ancient history scholar and atheist.

Discuss It!

1 Before you watched this video segment, what did you believe about the resurrection of Jesus? How was your view of the resurrection impacted by the segment? What questions did the segment raise for you?

2 William Craig lists five facts he believes point to the resurrection of Jesus as an actual event in history:

- Jesus of Nazareth was executed by crucifixion under Roman authority on the eve of Passover.
- Jesus' corpse was then laid in a tomb by Joseph of Arimathea, a delegate of the Jewish Sanhedrin that condemned Jesus.
- The tomb of Jesus was found empty on the Sunday morning following the crucifixion by a group of his women followers, including Mary Magdalene.
- Thereafter, various individuals and groups of people saw appearances of Jesus alive from the dead.
- The original disciples suddenly and sincerely came to believe in the resurrection of Jesus despite having every predisposition to the contrary.

Do you think these facts are sufficient pieces of evidence to support the resurrection as an actual event in history?

3 Richard Carrier argues that the empty tomb was first described in symbolic terms and later became misinterpreted as an actual event. Do you agree with Carrier's thinking? Why or why not?

"In a profound sense, Christianity without the resurrection is not simply Christianity without its final chapter. It is not Christianity at all."

Theologian Gerald O'Collins

4 Do you agree or disagree with Carrier's idea that if God really wanted to save all of humanity, he would not have sent his message of salvation "only in secret, to only a few people, only one time, two thousand years ago"? Explain your answer.

5 If God really did send Jesus into the world to be our Savior, what are some ways he could have made that unmistakably clear to everyone, but didn't? How would these ideas have impacted what people believed and didn't believe about Jesus?

6 Read the following eyewitness accounts from the New Testament of the post-resurrection appearances of Jesus:

Then the eleven disciples went to Galilee, to the mountain where Jesus had told them to go. When they saw him, they worshiped him; but some doubted. (Matthew 28:16–17)

When Jesus rose early on the first day of the week, he appeared first to Mary Magdalene, out of whom he had driven seven demons. She went and told those who had been with him and who were mourning and weeping. When they heard that Jesus was alive and that she had seen him, they did not believe it. (Mark 16:9–11)

Later Jesus appeared to the Eleven as they were eating; he rebuked them for their lack of faith and their stubborn refusal to believe those who had seen him after he had risen. (Mark 16:14)

While they were still talking about this, Jesus himself stood among them and said to them, "Peace be with you." They were startled and frightened, thinking they saw a ghost. He said to them, "Why are you troubled, and why do doubts rise in your minds? Look at my hands and my feet. It is I myself! Touch me and see; a ghost does not have flesh and bones, as you see I have." When he had said this, he showed them his hands and feet. And while they still did not believe it because of joy and amazement, he asked them, "Do you have anything here to eat?" They gave him a piece of broiled fish, and he took it and ate it in their presence. (Luke 24:36–43)

Early in the morning, Jesus stood on the shore, but the disciples did not realize it was Jesus. He called out to them, "Friends, haven't you any fish?" "No," they answered. He said, "Throw your net on the right side of the boat and you will find some." When they did, they were unable to haul the net in because of the large number of fish. Then the disciple whom Jesus loved said to Peter, "It is the Lord!" As soon as Simon Peter heard him say, "It is the Lord," he wrapped his outer garment around him (for he had taken it off) and jumped into the water. The other disciples followed in the boat.... When they landed, they saw a fire of burning coals there with fish on it, and some bread. Jesus said to them, "Bring some of the fish you have just caught." ... Jesus said to them, "Come and have breakfast. None of the disciples dared ask him, "Who are you?" They knew it was the Lord....

This was now the third time Jesus appeared to his disciples after he was raised from the dead." (John 21:4–10, 12–14)

For what I received I passed on to you as of first importance: that Christ died for our sins according to the Scriptures, that he was buried, that he was raised on the third day according to the Scriptures, and that he appeared to Cephas [Peter], and then to the Twelve. After that, he appeared to more than five hundred of the brothers and sisters at the same time, most of whom are still living.... Then he appeared to James, then to all the apostles, and last of all he appeared to me also. (Paul in 1 Corinthians 15:3–8)

What is your reaction to these verses? Why do you think some of the actual witnesses to Jesus' resurrection had difficulty believing even their own eyes?

> "It was therefore impossible that they [the early Christians] could have persisted in affirming the truths they have narrated, had not Jesus actually risen from the dead, and had they not known this fact as certainly as they knew any other fact."
>
> **Simon Greenleaf, an authority in jurisprudence at Harvard Law School**

7 Assuming the biblical accounts (see question 6) are accurate, does Dr. Craig's claim that the *diversity* of the resurrection appearances negates the possibility of the "hallucination theory"? Why or why not?

8 According to the following Scripture, what kind of evidence did it take for Thomas to believe that Jesus had risen from the dead? In what ways can you relate to Thomas? What kinds of evidence would it take for *you* to believe that the resurrection occurred?

> *Now Thomas (also known as Didymus), one of the Twelve, was not with the disciples when Jesus came. So the other disciples told him, "We have seen the Lord!" But he said to them, "Unless I see the nail marks in his hands and put my finger where the nails were, and put my hand into his side, I will not believe." A week later his disciples were in the house again, and Thomas was with them. Though the doors were locked, Jesus came and stood among them and said, "Peace be with you!" Then he said to Thomas, "Put your finger here; see my hands. Reach out your hand and put it into my side. Stop doubting and believe." Thomas said to him, "My Lord and my God!" Then Jesus told him, "Because you have seen me, you have believed; blessed are those who have not seen and yet have believed." (John 20:24–29)*

9 How would your beliefs about Jesus Christ be impacted if it were proven that Jesus never rose from the dead? Do you believe that the Christian faith hinges on the resurrection?

> "I know pretty well what evidence is, and I tell you, such evidence as that for the resurrection has never broken down yet."
>
> **John Singleton Copley, one of the greatest legal minds in British history**

10 In your opinion, what is the significance of the resurrection? Does it matter to you that Jesus rose from the dead?

> "If Christ has not been raised, your faith is futile; you are still in your sins."
>
> **Apostle Paul in 1 Corinthians 15:17**

11 What implications does the resurrection have for you? For example, how would your view of life, death, and the afterlife change if the resurrection has or has not occurred?

Watch It! Lee's Perspective

The evidence for the resurrection was pivotal in my decision to become a Christian. First, there's the empty tomb—everybody in the ancient world acknowledged it was vacant. The question was: how did it get empty? The authorities made up the absurd story that the disciples stole the body, but they [the disciples] clearly lacked motive or opportunity. Second, there are eyewitnesses. More than 515 individuals encountered the risen Jesus, and hardcore skeptics like James and Saul of Tarsus were transformed into believers. As British theologian Michael Green said, "The appearances of Jesus are as well authenticated as anything in antiquity.... There can be no rational doubt that they occurred." Third, there are early accounts that date back so close to the events that they cannot be the product of legendary development. And, fourth, there's the willingness of the disciples to die for their conviction that the crucified Jesus came back to life. They didn't just *believe* the resurrection was true; they were in a unique position to *know* firsthand that it actually occurred. Nobody knowingly and willingly dies for a lie. To me, the bottom line was this: anybody can claim to be the Son of God, but only Jesus proved it by conquering the grave.

Chart It!

At this point in your spiritual journey, what degree of certainty do you have that the resurrection actually occurred? On a 1–10 scale, place an X near the spot and phrase that best describes you. Share your selection with the rest of the group and give reasons for placing your X where you did.

1	2	3	4	5	6	7	8	9	10

I see no evidence for Jesus' resurrection.	Something very unusual happened back then, but I'm not sure what.	I believe Jesus rose from the dead as the early church claimed.

Study It!

Take some time later this week to check out what the Bible teaches about the resurrection.

- Mark 16:9–14
- Luke 24:13–53
- John 20:10–31
- John 21:1–25

DO ALL ROADS
LEAD TO GOD?

Read It!

One Way?

Jeff and Tony sat on the floor of their dorm room, staring at the open books in front of them.

"So ... what do you make of this, Jeff?" Tony asked.

"I don't know," Jeff muttered. "I didn't like it when you told me about it, and I don't like it any better reading it for myself."

"I know what you mean. You got another slice of pizza over there?"

"Here," Jeff slid the box over to his friend, the remaining piece of cold pepperoni pizza shifting during the transition. "Maybe it's not as bad as it sounds. Let me read it again." He picked up the Bible and read the troubling verse carefully: " 'Jesus answered, 'I am the way and the truth and the life. No one comes to the Father except through me.' Nope, it still sounds totally exclusive. I hate it."

"It doesn't sound like the gentle, loving Jesus that I remember hearing about growing up," Tony said.

"It seems like he's drawing a line in the sand. You're either in or out," Jeff complained.

"But ... what if that's it? What if he *is* the way, the *only* way?" Tony asked as he munched a bite of pizza.

"Look, maybe we've got it all wrong. Maybe it doesn't mean what we think it means. We need an expert," Jeff said.

"What time is it?" Tony asked, polishing off the last bite of crust.

"Late," Jeff observed.

"Let's just check out that church down on Third. Maybe somebody will still be around there."

"Why not?" Jeff agreed.

The door creaked as they slowly pushed it open. The pews were empty, the lights dim, the wooden floors echoed as they walked down the aisle. A moment later, someone in the back opened a door, spilling a ray of light into the sanctuary.

"Can I help you guys?" asked the slender, gray-haired man standing in the doorway.

"Yeah, sure, that would be great," Tony said as he introduced the two of them. "We were talking about a verse in the Bible, and we wanted another opinion. What do you make of this?" Tony flipped open his Bible to John 14:6 and read it aloud. "That sounds awfully exclusive. It doesn't seem fair to me to count some in and some out based on whether or not they happened to hear about Jesus."

The pastor—"just call me Stephen"—nodded; he had taught from this passage a few times in his thirty-plus years of ministry. "Jesus didn't mean he was the *only* way," he assured them. "He meant he was the *best* way. He was—and is—the *best* way to learn about the way to God."

Jeff shook his head. "But that's not what it says. Jesus is saying he is *the* way, and we need to find truth and life through him alone. Isn't that the point he's making?"

"Imagine taking a road trip to Chicago," Stephen began. "There are a lot of different highways and side roads you could take to get there. Some ways would take longer than others, but there *is* a best, most direct way. The best way is the most efficient way, but it's okay if you don't take the most efficient way, because all ways will eventually get you there." Stephen noticed Tony tapping the arm of his chair nervously. "What's on your mind, Tony?"

Tony stopped tapping. "I see your point, but some things *are* very narrow. Jeff's car runs only on gasoline, not water or milk or beer. We can't try pouring Mountain Dew in his gas tank because there's no other way to make his engine run so we can make the trip to Chicago in the first place. See, there's no give or take on some things. Look, Stephen, a lot of times, there really is only one way ... and maybe this time, Jesus meant he was *the* only way."

Stephen looked at the boys with compassion. He understood

their desire to find answers. It reminded him of his own search years ago, which led him into ministry. He wanted to encourage them. "Think about it—"

"I am!" Tony exclaimed. Jeff elbowed him.

"No, it's okay. I understand your excitement. Let me try explaining it this way. In science, the answers are often cut-and-dried, but in subjects like philosophy and theology, it's more interpretive, more fluid. So consider this: If you want to master a subject, say something like physics, you have a couple of ways to go about it. You could go to the bookstore and the library and gather a lot of books around you, read them all, and you'd probably learn a lot about physics. But another way," he leaned forward, hoping this analogy fit the undergrad mentality, "would be to sign up for a college course on physics taught by a brilliant professor. Now, you tell me, which of those two ways would be the *best* way to learn about physics?"

"Signing up for the course," Tony answered.

"Exactly." Stephen watched their faces. "That's what Jesus meant. Going to God through Jesus is like taking the course taught by the all-knowing master. He isn't the *only* way to God, but he *is* the *best* way."

Both Tony and Jeff hesitated, each deep in thought. Finally, Jeff broke the silence. "Thanks for your time, Stephen."

"No problem. Come back any time. Take care."

When the heavy door shut behind Jeff and Tony, they paused on the top step. "What's the matter, Jeff?" Tony asked.

"I don't know ... I guess I just wonder," Jeff continued, as they headed back to the dorm. "It still seems like he's changing the meaning. Hey, which way do you want to take back to the dorm?"

"I don't suppose it matters," Tony said with a grin. "Or does it?"

Watch It!

Use the following space to take notes as you view the video in which Lee Strobel interviews Kenneth Bowers, a member of the national governing body of the Baha'i of the United States and author of *God Speaks Again: An Introduction to the Baha'i Faith*, and Gregory Koukl, president of Stand to Reason and author of the book *Relativism: Feet Firmly Planted in Mid-Air*.

Discuss It!

1 Why do you think there are so many different religions in the world? Is it confusing or frustrating to you that there are so many religions from which to choose? Explain.

> "The soul of religions is one, but it is encased in a multitude of forms.... Truth is the exclusive property of no single scripture.... I cannot ascribe exclusive divinity to Jesus. He is as divine as Krishna or Rama or Mohammed or Zoroaster."
>
> **Mahatma Gandhi**

2 Why do you think God allows so many religions to exist? Why doesn't he just narrow down the choices so it's easier to find him?

3 Do you think all the major religions are fundamentally the same or fundamentally different? If you can, give reasons to back up your answer.

"I am absolutely against any religion that says that one faith is superior to another. I don't see how that is anything different than spiritual racism. It's a way of saying that we are closer to God than you, and that's what leads to hatred."
Rabbi Schmuley Boteach

4 Consider the following two statements: "There are many different ways to get to my house."/"All roads lead to my house." Are both of these statements logical? Why or why not?

"To overlook obvious differences between religions might seem broad-minded. In reality it is about as proud and narrow as a person could get. To say all religions are basically the same is to claim to be smarter than each of the billions of people who believe the unique aspects of their religion are of supreme importance to God. It is to claim that even though you are not an expert in their religion, you know they are wrong—you know their religion is really no different."
Grantley Morris

5 How likely does it seem to you that any one religion would have the final say on what is true or not? Explain.

> "The extreme [Christian] who believes that all Muslims go to hell is probably not so much ignorant ... as blinded by dark dogmatic spectacles through which he can see no good in religious devotion outside his own."
> **Theologian John Hick**

6 Kenneth Bowers holds to the Baha'i belief that there is one God who has progressively revealed the same path through various divine messengers throughout history (including, but not limited to, Buddha, Jesus, and Muhammad). What are some of the strengths and weaknesses of this claim? Do you agree or disagree with this assertion? Explain.

7 Given two contradictory and opposing statements, choose all that apply:

❑ Both statements may be true at the same time.
❑ Both statements cannot be true at the same time.
❑ At least one statement must be false.
❑ One statement may be true or both statements may be false, but both statements cannot both be true at the same time.

> "Moses could mediate on the law; Muhammad could brandish a sword; Buddha could give personal counsel; Confucius could offer wise sayings; but none of these men was qualified to offer an atonement for the sins of the world.... Christ alone is worthy of unlimited devotion and service."
> **Theologian R. C. Sproul**

8 Gregory Koukl makes the following statement: "Either Jesus was the Messiah or he was not the Messiah. If he's *not* the Messiah then the Jews are right and the Christians are wrong. If he *is* the Messiah then the Christians are right and the Jews are wrong. Under no circumstance can they both be right. When you die you either go to heaven or hell, or you get reincarnated, or you get absorbed into God, or you lie in the grave. But you can't do them all." What is your reaction to Koukl's statement? Does it seem reasonable to expect all religions to be true in their own way, in spite of significant differences? Why or why not? Explain your response.

9 Read the legend of the elephant and the blind men (see box, pages 54–55). How does this legend apply to the issue of searching for and discovering the truth about God and religion? Do you agree with its conclusion? Why or why not?

An Indian Legend
Six Blind Men and the Elephant

It was six men of Indostan
To learning much inclined,
Who went to see the Elephant
(Though all of them were blind),
That each by observation
Might satisfy his mind.
The First approached the Elephant,
And happening to fall
Against his broad and sturdy side,
At once began to bawl:
"God bless me! but the Elephant
Is very like a wall!"
The Second, feeling of the tusk,
Cried, "Ho! what have we here,
So very round and smooth and sharp?
To me 'tis mighty clear
This wonder of an Elephant
Is very like a spear!"
The Third approached the animal,
And happening to take
The squirming trunk within his hands,
Thus boldly up he spake:
"I see," quoth he, "the Elephant
Is very like a snake!"
The Fourth reached out an eager hand,
And felt about the knee:
"What most this wondrous beast is like
Is mighty plain," quoth he;
"'Tis clear enough the Elephant
Is very like a tree!"
The Fifth, who chanced to touch the ear,
Said: "E'en the blindest man

Can tell what this resembles most;
Deny the fact who can,
This marvel of an Elephant
Is very like a fan!"
The Sixth no sooner had begun
About the beast to grope,
Than, seizing on the swinging tail
That fell within his scope.
"I see," quoth he, "the Elephant
Is very like a rope!"
And so these men of Indostan
Disputed loud and long,
Each in his own opinion
Exceeding stiff and strong,
Though each was partly in the right,
They all were in the wrong!

JOHN GODFREY SAXE (1816–1887)

10 Do you agree or disagree with the concept that because human understanding is finite, and God is infinite, humans need some kind of divine revelation to more fully understand who God is, so that we are no longer like the "blind men" only seeing a small part of the larger truth? Explain your response.

11 According to the following Bible verses, do you think that Jesus taught that there are many paths to God? Explain.

[Jesus speaking] "Enter through the narrow gate. For wide is the gate and broad is the road that leads to destruction, and many enter through it. But small is the gate and narrow the road that

leads to life, and only a few find it. Watch out for false prophets. They come to you in sheep's clothing, but inwardly they are ferocious wolves." (Matthew 7:13–15)

For there is one God and one mediator between God and mankind, the man Christ Jesus, who gave himself as a ransom for all people. (1 Timothy 2:5–6)

Therefore Jesus said again, "Very truly I tell you, I am the gate for the sheep. All who have come before me are thieves and robbers, but the sheep have not listened to them. I am the gate; whoever enters through me will be saved. (John 10:7)

He [Jesus] was in the world, and though the world was made through him, the world did not recognize him. He came to that which was his own, but his own did not receive him. Yet to all who did receive him, to those who believed in his name, he gave the right to become children of God. (John 1:10–12)

There is a way that appears to be right, but in the end it leads to death. (Proverbs 14:12)

Jesus answered, "I am the way and the truth and the life. No one comes to the Father except through me." (John 14:6)

Jesus answered: "Watch out that no one deceives you. For many will come in my name, claiming, 'I am the Messiah,' and will deceive many.... At that time many will turn away from the faith and will betray and hate each other, and many false prophets will appear and deceive many people." (Matthew 24:4–5, 10–11)

12 According to the Scriptures from question 11, what conclusions can you draw about Jesus' claim to be the only way to God? How confident are you that all roads lead to God?

> "Even though many religions seem to be the same on the surface, the closer one gets to the central teachings, the more apparent the differences become. It is totally incorrect to say that all religions are the same."
>
> **Josh McDowell,** *Answers to Tough Questions*
> *Skeptics Ask about the Christian Faith*

13 How, if at all, do the exclusive claims of Jesus worry, bother, or embarrass you? Has your reaction changed over time? Explain.

Watch It! Lee's Perspective

I can certainly understand Ken Bowers' desire to interpret world religions in a way that diminishes their distinctions and downplays Jesus' claims to exclusivity. However, I agree with Greg Koukl—there are irreconcilable differences at the very foundations of the world's faiths. To give just three examples, polytheists believe there's a multiplicity of impersonal gods; Christians believe in one triune and personal God, with Jesus as God's only Son; Muslims specifically deny God's triune nature and Jesus' divinity. To gloss over these differences is to gut these religions of their essential beliefs. To me, Jesus' teachings are clear: he is the only way to God. Otherwise, his death on the cross would have been superfluous. The issue, then, becomes whether we can believe Jesus when he makes this remarkable claim. And that's where Jesus' credentials become important—his miracles, which were seen by eyewitnesses, including skeptics; his fulfillment of ancient prophecies against all mathematical odds; and his resurrection from the dead, which authenticated his claim to being the Son of God. In short, I believe Jesus backs up his identity unlike the leader of any other world religion. And that's what gives him unique credibility when he says he's the sole path to salvation.

Chart It!

At this point in your spiritual journey, do you believe religions are fundamentally the same or fundamentally different? On a 1–10 scale, place an X near the spot and phrase that best describes you. Share your selection with the rest of the group and give reasons for placing your X where you did.

1	2	3	4	5	6	7	8	9	10

I believe all religions are basically the same.	I'm not sure it's a good idea to even try to compare religions with each other.	Other religions may have some truth, but they are all very different.

Study It!

Take some time later this week to check out what the Bible teaches about various religious points of view.

- Matthew 7:13–27
- Matthew 22:1–14
- Matthew 25:31–46
- John 3:16
- John 14:6
- 1 John 5:20

IS THE BIBLE BOGUS?

Read It!

Holy Smoke?

Eric and Heather, a young couple in their twenties, came to the discussion group because their neighbor Ted invited them. Ben and Mei get a babysitter every week and ride their bikes a few minutes through the neighborhood to attend. Carol, a soft-spoken woman in her thirties, usually doesn't say much. She prefers to listen. "I'm just learning from you all," she frequently says. Nick and Stephanie keep things lively with their strong ideas about nearly every topic they've covered, and Peter facilitates the discussions to cover a variety of spiritual topics.

Last week, when they were discussing miracles, Nick threw out a challenge. "Peter," he said, "you're always using Bible verses for us to respond to, but I think the Bible is a pretty lousy resource book. Can we leave the Bible out of it?"

"I agree," said Ted, nodding.

"Me, too," Stephanie said. In fact, everyone seemed intensely interested in this issue.

"That's a good point," Peter agreed. "Would you like to discuss the credibility of the Bible next week?" Everyone agreed. "Okay, then. Come ready to bring your issues and questions about whether or not the Bible can be trusted."

"That shouldn't be a problem," Nick said. "It won't take me any prep time at all. I can tell you right here and now everything that bugs me."

Peter laughed. "That's great—at least we're guaranteed an energetic start to our discussion!"

When they gathered the next week, Nick started. "Listen, I've read the Bible from cover to cover in five and a half months, and it's a very scary book."

"Tell me more," Peter urged.

"Don't get him started!" Ted exclaimed.

Nick grinned. "Ted and I have had some conversations about

this over coffee. Okay, for one thing, the Bible is full of disturbing contradictions. It says, 'Thou shall not kill,' yet the Israelites said that God told them to wipe out an entire group of people. So you tell me how that can translate into a clear set of principles for me to follow!"

Eric jumped in. "Personally, I think that the Bible has some truth to it, but it's also full of errors ... the trick is figuring out which part is which."

"Well, that brings up something I wanted to point out," Ted interjected. "I think the Bible was written by humans, but Christians try to tell us that it's written by God. Then they turn right around and use it to manipulate and justify hurting people in the name of God. I hate that. I think it was written by people, and that it's totally impossible for a group of imperfect people to write a completely perfect book. The Bible may have some remarkable wisdom here and there, but it didn't come from God. It is a mixture of human truth and error."

"Good point," Nick affirmed. "I agree with that."

"I wonder why people think the Bible is better than any other holy book?" Stephanie proposed. "There are so many sacred writings; shouldn't we treat them all with the same degree of respect and care?"

"Whoa, slow down!" Peter exclaimed. He was scribbling notes on a piece of paper. "You've brought up so many great points. Should we stop and discuss any of them in detail? I'm trying to keep up."

"No, I think we should get it all out on the table and then deal with them one by one," Nick stated. "So, Peter, here's another one for you to add to your list: people need to read the Bible critically, and I just don't see Christians doing that. They're so gullible."

"Well, where I come from, as a Buddhist, I was forbidden to read the Bible," Mei explained. "It's considered to be an evil book. But now that we've been referencing it in our group discussions, I've gotten to where I want to read it for myself to see if there's any truth to that."

"Don't bother," Nick said. "I just read it, and trust me: it's evil."

"Do you mean that?" Carol said. Everyone turned their attention to her. "Do you really and truly think it's evil, Nick?"

"Well, yeah, pretty much," he answered.

"Why do you ask, Carol?" Peter asked.

Carol stopped fiddling with the fringe of a pillow. "Well, I've been listening to all of you, and I love your ideas. I think you've brought up some great points, but I have to say one thing about the Bible. I've never thought it was evil, but I did think it was outdated and irrelevant. But then, like you, Nick, I decided to read it in the past few months, and it blew my mind. It's nothing like what I thought it was. It's as relevant as any self-help, philosophy, or religious book written today."

There was a pause in the flow of conversation. Carol rarely spoke her mind this firmly. "Thanks for sharing your opinion, Carol," Peter finally said, breaking the silence.

"Yeah," Nick said. "We're all entitled to our point of view."

Ben said, "Have you noticed that people interpret different passages all different ways? Who do we believe? Anyone can make the Bible say whatever they want, so how do we know what the authors of the Bible really intended to say?"

"Good question," Nick agreed. "A very good question."

Heather looked up. "Yeah, how do know for sure *what* the Bible says?"

Watch It!

Use the following space to take notes as you view the video in which Lee Strobel interviews Dr. Michael Shermer, founding publisher of *Skeptic* magazine and author of several books, including *How We Believe*, and Dr. Ben Witherington III, a New Testament scholar at Asbury Seminary and the author of more than twenty books and commentaries, including the award-winning *The Jesus Quest*.

Discuss It!

1 Name a book you have recently read and would recommend to others. What did you like about it? What do you think are the top bestselling books of all time? Where does the Bible rank on your list?

2 Growing up, what do you remember hearing or believing about the Bible? Were you an "easy sell" or were you convinced the Bible was "bogus"? Explain your answer. How, if at all, has your view of the Bible changed over the years?

3 Which of the following statements best describe your current view of the Bible?

❑ The Bible should be accepted as true by faith and without reservation.

❑ The Bible must be substantiated with convincing evidence.

❑ The Bible is filled with lots of contradictions.

❑ The Bible is outdated and irrelevant.

❑ The Bible should be scrutinized, but ultimately we must accept that there are some things about the Bible that we will never fully understand.

❑ The Bible has a lot of wisdom but that doesn't mean it's from God.

❑ The Bible is a mixture of truth and human error.

"What I'm saying is, if God wanted to send us a message, and ancient writings were the only way he could think of doing it, he could have done a better job."

Dr. Arroway in Carl Sagan's *Contact*

4 Do you believe the Gospels are reliable or do they report mostly what the authors and others merely wish was true? Explain.

5 Michael Shermer is convinced the Bible is "myth history," and Ben Witherington says the ancient Jews were not myth-making people but intended to report only what had actually occurred. Based on what you've read of the Gospels, who do you think is right? Why?

"Above all, you must understand that no prophecy of Scripture came about by the prophet's own interpretation of things. For prophecy never had its origin in the human will, but prophets, though human, spoke from God as they were carried along by the Holy Spirit."

2 Peter 1:20–21

6 Dr. Shermer argues that the Bible cannot be used to prove itself and that outside sources must be examined. Give reasons why you agree or disagree with him.

7 Which of the following four types of evidence—eyewitness accounts, numerous ancient manuscripts, archaeological findings, accurate prophetic predictions—if substantiated, would be the most compelling arguments for the credibility of the Bible? Why?

8 What specific errors, contradictions, or inaccuracies have you found in the Bible?

"I've made a hobby of collecting alleged discrepancies, inaccuracies, and conflicting statements in the Bible. I have a list of about eight hundred of them. A few years ago I coauthored a book called *When Critics Ask*, which devotes nearly six hundred pages to setting the record straight. All I can tell you is that in my experience when critics raise these objections, they invariably violate one of seventeen principles for interpreting Scripture."

Norman Geisler, PhD

9 Shermer shares that he does not believe in such things as the paranormal or the supernatural, only in the normal and natural. What about you? What do you believe about the supernatural? Give reasons for your response. Do you think it's more reasonable to (1) rule out the possibility of the supernatural at the outset, or (2) follow the evidence of science and history wherever they lead, even if they point toward the existence of the supernatural? Why?

10 To what extent do you believe that God has communicated to human beings through the Bible? Explain your response. What might be some possible obstacles to such a feat?

Inspiration of the Bible

Christians don't believe God literally dictated the Bible's contents. However, they do believe that the Bible contains the inspired Word of God.

Here's how biblical scholar Charles C. Ryrie explained it: "Inspiration is ... God's superintendence of the human authors so that, using their own individual personalities, they composed and recorded without error his revelation to man in the words of the original autographs."

Ryrie said that the Bible "tells the truth. Truth can and does include approximations, free quotations, language of appearances, and different accounts of the same event as long as those do not contradict."

11 Charles Ryrie believes the Bible "tells the truth" (see box, page 69). What does he mean by this statement? Do you agree with it? Why or why not?

12 Share your responses to the following:

• Something that surprises me about the Bible that I didn't really realize before this discussion is:

• A new question I have about the Bible that this discussion has surfaced is:

• Something that remains troublesome to me about the Bible is:

> "All Scripture is God-breathed and is useful for teaching, rebuking, correcting and training in righteousness, so that the servant of God may be thoroughly equipped for every good work."
>
> **2 Timothy 3:16**

13 What would it take for you to place confidence in the Bible as truth from God and as the supreme guide for your life?

14 What practical difference would it make in your everyday experience to believe that the Bible is God's Word?

Watch It! Lee's Perspective

For years, I was a skeptic about the Bible—not because I had thoroughly studied it and concluded it was unreliable, but because I had heard enough snippets of criticism through the years to poison my view of the book. It wasn't until I analyzed the Bible thoroughly that I concluded it must have a divine origin.

Not only is its wisdom—particularly expressed in the Proverbs, the Psalms, and Jesus' teachings—breathtaking in its beauty and depth, but the Bible is based on key eyewitness accounts; it has been repeatedly corroborated by archaeological discoveries; it has specific predictions that were made hundreds of years in advance and that were literally fulfilled against all mathematical odds; and it contains credible and well-documented miracles that confirm its message. The New Testament's historical reliability, as I describe in my book *The Case for Christ*, is especially well-established, and the unprecedented proliferation of ancient manuscripts provides confidence that the Bible was accurately transmitted to us over the centuries.

So let me ask this: do you know of any other book that matches its credentials?

Chart It!

At this point in your spiritual journey, what do you believe about the Bible? On a 1–10 scale, place an X near the spot and phrase that best describes you. Share your selection with the rest of the group and give reasons for placing your X where you did.

1	2	3	4	5	6	7	8	9	10

I'm not
convinced
the whole Bible
is from God.

I'm unsure
what to
believe about
the Bible.

I'm convinced
the Bible—
all of it—
is God's Word.

Study It!

Take some time later this week to check out what the Bible teaches about the reliability of its Scriptures.

- Psalm 18:30
- Psalm 33:4
- Psalm 119
- 2 Timothy 3:16
- Hebrews 4:12
- 2 Peter 1:20–21

DOES SCIENCE
POINT TOWARD
A CREATOR?

session 6

Read It!

No Evidence?

"For those who believe in God, no explanation is necessary. For those who do not, no explanation is possible."

Opening lines of the film *The Song of Bernadette*

"I don't know if God exists, but it would be better for his reputation if he didn't."

Jules Renard, French writer

"If God did not exist it would be necessary to invent him."

Voltaire

"There cannot be a God because if there were one, I could not believe that I was not he."

Friedrich Nietzsche

"People see God every day, they just don't recognize him."

Pearl Bailey

"I cannot imagine how the clockwork of the universe can exist without a clockmaker."

Voltaire

"I'd have to say that the biggest reason why I don't believe in god is because there is no proof of his existence. Throughout the millions of years that man has been on earth, there has never been any solid evidence that there is a creator. If there is a god, wouldn't he want as many followers as possible? Why leave any doubt? Why not come to earth and tell everyone he exists? Or, better yet, make it so that everyone knows he is there."

Norm, in an online discussion

"Those who turn to God for comfort may find comfort but I do not think they will find God."

Mignon McLaughlin, *The Neurotic's Notebook*

"My studies in Speculative philosophy, metaphysics, and science are all summed up in the image of a mouse called man running in and out of every hole in the Cosmos hunting for the Absolute Cheese."

Benjamin De Casseres, American poet, 1873–1945

"I do not believe in a personal God and I have never denied this but have expressed it clearly. If something is in me which can be called religious then it is the unbounded admiration for the structure of the world so far as our science can reveal it."

Albert Einstein in a letter dated March 24, 1954

"I didn't see any God out there."

Yuri Gagarin, Soviet cosmonaut,
after orbiting Earth

"God doesn't exist. Only silly, ignorant old women believe in him."

Ukrainian schoolteacher

"All I have seen teaches me to trust the Creator for all I have not seen."

Ralph Waldo Emerson

"I do not feel obliged to believe that the same God who has endowed us with sense, reason, and intellect has intended us to forgo their use."

Galileo

"The probability of life originating from accident is comparable to the probability of the unabridged dictionary resulting from an explosion in a printing factory."

Professor Edwin Conklin, Princeton University biologist

"Although science may solve the problem of how the universe began, it cannot answer the question: why does the universe bother to exist? I don't know the answer to that."

Steven Hawking

"Ironically, the picture of the universe bequeathed to us by the most advanced twentieth-century science is closer in spirit to the vision presented in the Book of Genesis than anything offered by science since Copernicus."

Dr. Patrick Glynn, atheist-turned-Christian

"Proof is only applicable to very rarefied areas of philosophy and mathematics.... For the most part we are driven to acting on good evidence, without the luxury of proof. There is good evidence of the link between cause and effect. There is good evidence that the sun will rise tomorrow. There is good reason to believe that I am the same man as I was ten years ago. There is good reason to believe my mother loves me and is not just fattening me up for the moment when she will pop arsenic into my tea. And there is good reason to believe in God. Very good reason. Not conclusive proof, but very good reason just the same.... I believe it is much harder to reject the existence of a supreme being than accept it."

Michael Green, *Faith for the Non-religious*

"God, were he all-powerful and perfectly good, would have created a world in which there was no unnecessary evil.... It has been contended that there is evil in this world—unnecessary evil—and that the more popular and philosophically more significant of the many attempts to explain this evil are completely unsatisfactory. Hence we must conclude from the existence of evil that there cannot be an omnipotent, benevolent God."

J. McCloskey, *God and Evil*

"Our personal concept of God—when we pray, for instance—is *worthless* unless it coincides with his revelation of himself."

Paul E. Little, *Know What You Believe*

"Religion is something left over from the infancy of our intelligence; it will fade away as we adopt reason and science as our guidelines."

Bertrand Russell

"God gave us ... two powerful and well-matched abilities: to prove things we find hard to believe and to believe in things we find hard to prove."

Michael Guillen, *Can a Smart Person Believe in God?*

"Question boldly even the existence of God."

Thomas Jefferson

"The best data we have (concerning the origin of the universe) are exactly what I would have predicted, had I nothing to go on but the five books of Moses, the Psalms, and the Bible as a whole."

Nobel-winning physicist Arno Penzias

"The whole point of faith is to believe regardless of the evidence, which is the very antithesis of science."

Michael Shermer, publisher, *Skeptic* magazine

"The exquisite order displayed by our scientific understanding of the physical world calls for the divine."

Dr. Vera Kistiakowski,
former professor of physics at MIT

"Charles Darwin didn't want to murder God, as he once put it. But he did."

Time magazine

So what do *you* say? Does God exist or not? Some people believe with certainty that he does, while others believe with equal certainty that he doesn't. Many others live with ambivalence. With so many compelling and contradictory ideas out there, how does anyone really know *what* to believe?

Watch It!

Use the following space to take notes as you view the video in which Lee Strobel interviews Dr. Stephen Meyer, director of the Center for Science and Culture at Seattle's Discovery Institute and coauthor of *Darwinism, Design, and Public Education*, and Dr. Michael Shermer, publisher of *Skeptic* magazine and author of *The Science of Good and Evil*.

Discuss It!

1 Do you believe there is a God or some kind of Intelligent Designer behind the origin of the universe? Why or why not?

2 Growing up, what did you learn about evolution? Did that influence your beliefs about God? How so?

3 Which of the following arguments by Dr. Stephen Meyer do you think best or least supports the argument for an Intelligent Designer? Do you think these reasons are sufficient to support the intelligent design theory? Explain your answer.

- ❑ The universe had a beginning and therefore must have had a cause.
- ❑ The universe is so finely tuned that if it were different in infinitesimally minor ways, it would be impossible for life to exist.
- ❑ The high-tech information processing "machinery" being discovered by biologists in the lowest forms of life is too intricate and complex to have happened by chance and must have originated from some form of intelligence.
- ❑ Nature can produce patterns but not information. All information—whether in a book, drawing, or computer code—has an intelligent source. Therefore, the biological information in DNA, which uses a four-character chemical alphabet to spell out the precise assembly instructions for

all the proteins out of which living things are built, must have its roots in an intelligence.

4 Michael Shermer counters that the "default answer" to Meyer's points is *not* that there must be a designer, creator, or god behind the universe, but rather, it is perfectly acceptable in science to conclude "we don't know." Do you agree? Why or why not?

5 Shermer addresses Meyer's first point that something that begins to exist needs a creator by arguing that if God does not need a creator, then the universe itself does not need a creator. Do you agree or disagree with this line of reasoning? Explain.

"An atheist is a man who believes himself an accident."
Francis Thompson

6 Both Shermer and Meyer agree that the universe is designed, but one difference between them is how *well* it is designed. Shermer believes the universe is a tinkered patchwork, and not very well designed. Meyer disagrees and states that the universe is exquisitely designed. Who do you think is right? Give reasons for your response.

7 True or false: Everything that begins to exist *must* have a cause. True or false: Where there is design, there *must* be a designer. Give reasons for your answer.

"If there were no God, there would be no atheists."
G. K. Chesterton

8 Suppose, for a moment, that the intelligent design theory is correct. How would you answer Shermer's question, "Who created the intelligent creator?" Explain your response.

9 Shermer rules out the possibility of the supernatural at the outset. Two-time Nobel Prize-winner Linus Pauling said: "Science is the search for the truth." If Pauling is right, should scientists be free to consider the possibility of the supernatural if the evidence of cosmology, physics, and biochemistry point in that direction? Why or why not?

10 Meyer believes it's contradictory to say that God guides an inherently unguided natural process or that God designed a natural mechanism as a substitute for his design. Read the following Bible verses and other quotations. Do you think it is possible to believe in Darwinian evolution and still be a Christian? In other words, does Darwinism explain away the need for a Creator? Explain your answer.

> *"By faith we understand that the universe was formed at God's command, so that what is seen was not made out of what was visible." (Hebrews 11:3)*

> *"In the beginning God created the heavens and the earth. Now the earth was formless and empty, darkness was over the surface of the deep, and the Spirit of God was hovering over the waters. And God said, 'Let there be light,' and there was light." (Genesis 1:1–3)*

> *"For since the creation of the world God's invisible qualities — his eternal power and divine nature — have been clearly seen, being understood from what has been made [that is, his creation], so that people are without excuse." (Romans 1:20)*

"By coupling undirected, purposeless variation to the blind, uncaring process of natural selection, Darwin made theological or spiritual explanations of life processes superfluous."

Evolutionary Biology

"[Darwin's] greatest accomplishment [was to show that] living beings can be explained as the result of a natural process, natural selection, without any need to resort to a Creator or other external agent."

Evolutionist Francisco Ayala

"A widespread theological view now exists saying that God started off the world, props it up and works through laws of nature, very subtly, so subtly that its action is undetectable. But that kind of God is effectively no different to my mind than atheism."

Evolutionist William Provine

"The whole point of Darwinism is to show that there is no need for a supernatural creator, because natural can do the creating by itself."

Phillip Johnson, author, *Darwin on Trial*

"You can have God *or* natural selection, but not both.... If we admit God into the process, Darwin argued, then God would ensure that only 'the right variations occurred ... and natural selection would be superfluous.'"

Nancy Pearcey

"I do not believe in God because I don't believe in Mother Goose."

Clarence Darrow

11 Do all scientists have motives? What are some examples? Are motives relevant in assessing the validity of scientific theories or can the data speak for themselves?

"Eighty-six percent of all Americans believe in God or a supreme being."

George magazine

12 To what extent do you think that science and Christianity are compatible? Explain.

13 Share some of the concrete reasons you have now for your belief—or disbelief—in the existence of God.

Watch It! Lee's Perspective

One of the main reasons I became an atheist was because of the theory of evolution I was taught in school. My conclusion was that if chemical evolution can explain the origin of life and if neo-Darwinism could explain its development and diversity, then God was clearly out of a job!

Ironically, though, even though my road to atheism was paved by science, so was my later journey to God. As I delved much deeper into the data, I found myself agreeing with hundreds of scientists—with doctorates from Cambridge, Stanford, Yale, Cornell, Rutgers, Chicago, Princeton, Berkeley, and other prestigious universities—who have publicly declared their skepticism over the grandest claims of Darwin.

On the positive side, I learned that a series of scientific discoveries over the last fifty years in a wide range of disciplines—from cosmology, physics, and astronomy to biochemistry, genetics, and human consciousness—point powerfully and persuasively toward the existence of a Creator. I ended up writing a book, *The Case for a Creator*, to describe the evidence that I found the most convincing.

Ultimately, I found myself agreeing with Dr. James Tour, the noted nanoscientist from Rice University, who said: "Only a rookie who knows nothing about science would say science takes away from faith. If you really study science, it will bring you closer to God."

Chart It!

At this point in your spiritual journey, what do you believe about the existence of a Creator God? On a 1–10 scale, place an X near the spot and phrase that best describes you. Share your selection with the rest of the group and give reasons for placing your X where you did.

1	2	3	4	5	6	7	8	9	10

I'm not convinced that an Intelligent Designer created the universe.	I'm unsure what to believe on how the universe came into existence.	I'm convinced that God exists and that he created the universe.

Study It!

Take some time later this week to check out what the Bible teaches about God's existence and how the universe came to be.

- Genesis 1
- Job 38–42
- Psalm 14:1
- Psalm 19:1–3
- Romans 1:18–32
- Hebrews 11:1–3

IS ANYTHING BEYOND FORGIVENESS?

Read It!

Keeping Score?

I wonder if God bothers to keep track of how well human beings perform here on earth. If he does, it seems like he would need a massive computer with sophisticated software to help him remember how we're doing. Maybe he uses a point system to track sins. If that's the case, he's probably got a complex mathematical formula to calculate all the trouble we cause.

So what's God's scheme? Maybe something like this: There are little sins—can they even be counted as *real* sins?—like telling a white lie to make someone feel better about her bad hair day or sharing a bit of gossip picked up at the water cooler to satisfy someone's curiosity. No one seems too alarmed by these indiscretions— there's no harm done here. The tracking system might assign only a few points to those "mistakes." Let's say they get a 1 or 2. You're only in trouble when you get a lot of them piled up over time.

The points start to add up more quickly with weightier sins. Think back to when you lied to your seventh-grade teacher to get out of detention, peeked at Sally Goodman's test answers during Chemistry, or stole a candy bar from the soccer snack bar. Those should get more points than a white lie. Let's say you earn 10, 12, or 14 points for those.

Then there are those arguable sins, the things that one person sees as a sin and another person laughs about as nothing. What about eating ten more crab legs at the all-you-can-eat seafood buffet, even though you weren't hungry: One person calls it gluttony—35 points?—while someone else calls it a great deal for the money—no points, only calories!

You called someone a name that shouldn't be repeated in mixed company. You noticed that the person felt wounded. What do you think, maybe a 56? But then if you were to actually hit or punch a person, how much worse would that be? 62 points? Unless you're boxing, of course—that's zero.

Then there are the big ones. How about stealing stuff worth over a thousand dollars? What about sleeping with someone else's husband? Are those in the upper 90s? They'd better be!

What about murder? How many points represent a life? Nothing less than a thousand points in my book.

Then again, maybe God should add another scale to track all the good things we do to bring our points down. It would be only fair—just like our court system, where we pay our debt to society by reimbursing for damages or doing time according to the enormity of our crime. Maybe if we sing Christmas carols at the nursing home, we bring our total down 10 points. Volunteer at a soup kitchen and watch the number drop 20 points. Smile at someone for 2, maybe 3 if that person smiles back. Move to Africa and work for a volunteer relief organization for a whopping 90 points per year.

It would be cool if we could simply do some kind of penance for our wrongdoings and hopefully bring those points down low enough to earn our way back into God's favor. How low do our points have to be to be good enough? Wow, if it has to be zero, we should really get busy.

Of course, as convenient as a point system would be, maybe it doesn't work like that at all. Maybe we have to feel really, really sorry, then beg and plead for God's forgiveness, all the while hoping that he's in a really, really good mood when we ask.

Or, wouldn't it be nice if God just completely forgave us, once and for all, whether we asked him to or not? That would be great, for me. I mean, I hope it doesn't work that way for Hitler, or my high school English teacher who gave me a D on my paper just because I was a week late—after all, creativity takes time. Maybe some people should have to work a little harder at earning forgiveness, but I like that system for me.

I wonder if God would ever be so loving, so kind, to offer us forgiveness with no strings attached, no points to redeem? Yep, now that would be *real* good.

Watch It!

Use the following space to take notes as you view the video in which Lee Strobel interviews Dr. Henry Cloud, clinical psychologist and bestselling author of *Boundaries, Changes That Heal,* and *Nine Things You Simply Must Do to Succeed in Love and Life,* and Father Frank Pavone, a prominent Roman Catholic priest, head of Priests for Life, and coauthor of *Rachel, Weep No More: How Divine Mercy Heals the Effects of Abortion.*

Discuss It!

1 Which is more difficult: to unconditionally forgive or to humbly ask for forgiveness? Why is forgiveness sometimes so hard for people to extend or receive?

2 What is your reaction to the idea that God forgives what human beings find unforgivable? Why is this concept hard to grasp or accept?

3 Father Pavone believes that God's forgiveness is not automatic, but rather it comes to those who repent and once true repentance is in place, there is no sin that God is unwilling to forgive. Do you believe people need to ask God for forgiveness in order to be forgiven or are they forgiven whether they ask for it or not? Explain your response.

> "The symbol of the religion of Jesus is the cross, not the scales."
>
> **British pastor John Stott**

4 Why would God refuse to forgive someone with an unrepentant heart? How is this similar or dissimilar to human forgiveness?

5 Both Father Pavone and Dr. Cloud believe that if Adolf Hitler were to have confessed his sins and asked God for forgiveness for the Holocaust, God would have wiped his slate clean. What is your reaction to that claim? Is God's mercy too great? Why or why not?

6 David Berkowitz, the "Son of Sam" serial killer serving life in prison, now claims to be a Christian. On what basis do you think he is or is not forgiven? Explain your response.

"Forgiveness is the answer to the child's dream of a miracle by which what is broken is made whole again, what is soiled is again made clean."
Nobel-winning statesman Dag Hammarskjold

7 To what extent do you believe God is willing to forgive people for the wrong that they do? In other words, is God willing to forgive everything, no matter what, or are there limits to what he is willing to forgive and forget?

8 Dr. Cloud claims that because God himself, in the form of Jesus, died for our sins, the size of the payment was enormous enough to cover every possible sin. Do you agree or disagree with this claim? Why?

9 What do you believe it means to repent? Does repentance begin with a *decision* or an *action*? Explain. How is repentance different from simply feeling badly about one's misdeeds or just saying "I'm sorry"?

10 What's the difference between a person who expects or demands forgiveness and a person who is sincerely sorry and genuinely asks for forgiveness?

11 Dr. Cloud warns that God's forgiveness is not "cheap;" in other words, people shouldn't attempt to take advantage of God's grace by thinking they can commit whatever sins they want and God will just forgive them. Do you agree with this line of reasoning? Why or why not? What's to prevent someone from saying: "I can do anything I want; God will forgive me no matter what"?

> "Look once again to Jesus Christ in his death upon the cross. Look and try to understand that what he did and suffered, he did and suffered for you, for me, for us all. He carried our sin, our captivity and our suffering, and did not carry it in vain. He carried it away."
>
> **Theologian Karl Barth**

12 According to the following verses, to what extent do you think the Bible teaches that we *earn* God's forgiveness? What exactly must we do to receive God's forgiveness?

> For it is by grace you have been saved, through faith — and this is not from yourselves, it is the gift of God — not by works, so that no one can boast. (Ephesians 2:8–9)

> Repent, then, and turn to God, so that your sins may be wiped out, that times of refreshing may come from the Lord (Acts 3:19)

> "The time has come," [Jesus] said. "The kingdom of God is near. Repent and believe the good news!" (Mark 1:15)

> If we confess our sins, he is faithful and just and will forgive us our sins and purify us from all unrighteousness. (1 John 1:9)

If you declare with your mouth, "Jesus is Lord," and believe in your heart that God raised him from the dead, you will be saved. For it is with your heart that you believe and are justified, and it is with your mouth that you profess your faith and are saved. (Romans 10:9–10)

13 Father Pavone suggests that blasphemy of the Holy Spirit, the one unforgivable sin, is refusing to repent. Cloud says that the unforgivable sin is refusing God's offer of forgiveness through Jesus Christ. What do you understand the unforgivable sin to be? Why would our rejection of God's offer of forgiveness through the death of his Son be unforgivable?

Watch It! Lee's Perspective

One of the most profound and breathtaking teachings of the Bible is that God offers complete and total forgiveness as a gift to anyone who seeks it in repentance and faith. Sometimes people think God's forgiveness is limited or small, because they mistakenly think his clemency is like human forgiveness. But clearly it's not:

- People are often reluctant to forgive, but Psalm 86:5 says, "You, Lord, are forgiving and good, abounding in love to all who call to you."
- People forgive but don't forget, yet Isaiah 43:25 says, "I, even I, am he who blots out your transgressions, for my own sake, and remembers your sins no more."
- People forgive minor annoyances but sometimes refuse to pardon major hurts. But Isaiah 1:18 assures us, "Though your sins are like scarlet, they shall be as white as snow; though they are red as crimson, they shall be like wool."
- People put conditions on their forgiveness. But Isaiah 55:7 says, "Let the wicked forsake their ways and the unrighteous their thoughts. Let them turn to the LORD, and he will have mercy on them, and to our God, for he will freely pardon."
- People may forgive one or two mistakes, but then draw the line. However, Lamentations 3:21–23 says, "Yet this I call to mind and therefore I have hope: Because of the LORD's great love we are not consumed, for his compassions never fail. They are new every morning; great is your faithfulness."
- People forgive but hold a grudge. "For I will forgive their wickedness," the Lord said in Jeremiah 31:34, "and will remember their sins no more."

Throughout history, the size of people's sin has never been the issue with God; the issue has always been whether people were willing to humble themselves and come clean with him about their guilt.

Personally, I can't help but love a God like that.

Chart It!

At this point in your spiritual journey, what do you believe about God's forgiveness? On a 1–10 scale, place an X near the spot and phrase that best describes you. Share your selection with the rest of the group and give reasons for placing your X where you did.

1	2	3	4	5	6	7	8	9	10

I'm not convinced that God has forgiven me.

I'm unsure what to believe about God's willingness or ability to forgive me.

I'm convinced that God has forgiven me through the payment Jesus made on my behalf.

Study It!

Take some time later this week to check out what the Bible teaches about God's forgiveness.

- Luke 15:3–7
- John 1:12
- John 3:1–18
- Acts 26:20
- Ephesians 1:3–8
- Ephesians 2:1–5
- 2 Timothy 1:8–10
- Titus 3:3–8

WHY DOES
GOD ALLOW
PAIN AND
SUFFERING?

Read It!

Had Enough?

"My name is Brenda, and I have had a hard life, filled with chaos, turmoil, and pain. I know other people have gone through horrible things much worse than I have, but this is my life. The words I use won't come close to fully describing all that I've gone through. You merely read these words, but I lived them.

"To say that my mother was a paranoid schizophrenic is hard enough, but to have actually grown up in her household was a nightmare. To tell you that my husband was an alcoholic for twenty years is one thing, but to have actually lived in that environment is quite another. But I'm getting ahead of myself.

"I was born in the Midwest. When I was six weeks old, my mom and dad separated, so I never knew my dad. I saw him on only two or three occasions. My parents divorced when I was two.

"When I was three years old, I was molested by a neighbor. When I was four, I was molested by a relative, and at the age of eight, I was molested again, this time by another relative. To this day, I have haunting pictures of these horrible things flowing through my mind.

"When I was ten, my mother was diagnosed with paranoid schizophrenia. She was hospitalized for six weeks and given shock treatments. Her memory was affected, and when she came home she didn't remember my name. Sometimes she would wake up in the middle of the night screaming. One time, when she was really sick, she couldn't speak for months.

"Because of the situation at home, I started dating when I was thirteen—too young, I know—and at the age of fifteen, I found myself pregnant. I lost the baby at six months—she only lived four hours. I got married at nineteen and had a son. The next year, I had a daughter.

"In September 1971, my husband, a truck driver, had a serious accident. He was in the hospital for a month in a body cast. He couldn't work for a year and we were on welfare.

"After his recovery, I followed my intuition one night and discovered his semi parked behind a bowling alley. When I opened the cab door I caught him having sex with a woman. I forgave him. I thought, *I have two little kids; I can get through this*. It's not easy when you know your husband is having an affair, but when you *see* it, well, it's very hard to endure. He promised not to do it again, but that didn't hold true. Things just got worse, so I decided to get a divorce and find a job.

"Later, I married again. My second husband had five children, and we had one child together. I basically raised the children alone, because he was an alcoholic. It was a rough road. Before we married I knew he drank, but I didn't know it was this bad.

"Our marriage was in constant turmoil. I can remember checking on him one night—my woman's intuition again—and sure enough, there he was, in the pickup truck with a woman. I filed for divorce.

"One summer, there was a tragedy with a little girl who lived across the street. She was friends with my kids. She was going to spend the night with us. She came in the house as I was making dinner. She said, 'I need to go back home and put my puppy back in the yard.' I should have said, 'No, sit down and eat. Dinner's ready, you can do it later.' Instead, I let her go.

"As she crossed the street, she was hit by a car and killed. I always felt responsible. Her parents ended up getting a divorce—this was their baby. I stayed in touch with her mother for a long time, because when you go through something like that you're connected for life. That was really hard.

"My father and mother had been divorced for years. They both died on the same day in 1999—ironically, it was their wedding anniversary. Then in 2001, my son suffered a head injury in an accident at his job site. To this day, he's in a persistent vegetative state. I visit him daily and take care of him. He constantly has infections and illnesses. When I walk in his room and say his name, he'll close his eyes so I know he's in there, but he's trapped. He hears my voice, and I know he knows.

"I've dealt with this for four years. People say, 'Why don't you take him off life support and let him go?' But he can breathe on his own right now, so that wouldn't be enough. I'd have to take him off the feeding tube, and that's something I can't do.

"When I didn't think things in my life could get any worse, my daughter was found dead in her bed the day after Mother's Day. She was only thirty-seven. We have no idea what she died from. The autopsy came back with no answers. The toxicology report was inconclusive. We will probably never have any real closure. She left four children.

"These last four years—with the loss of my children—have been the worst. I'm stressed, worried, and worn out. When I look back on my life, though, I have to admit that a lot of the hardship I brought on myself by the poor choices I've made. It's like a chain reaction. I used to tell my children and grandchildren, 'Just think carefully about the choices you make. Everything you do in your life—every single decision—means so much.'

"I have one daughter left now. She just turned thirty. She has two girls and a new baby boy. They are beautiful and healthy. She had her baby a week early, thankfully, because a week later, her stepsister died. Now there is little joy with this new baby—you lose a life, you gain a life. It will take a while before she gets over this most recent loss. She feels like something evil is all around us. With her sister dying and her brother's accident, she's wondering if she's next—we're all terrified.

"I know everybody goes through difficulties—life is hard, very hard. But this is what I've experienced. I wonder where God has been through all this. Did I push him out of the way, or did he leave on his own? Either way, I don't sense that he's been around much. And yet, I guess down deep in my heart I know that he's been there for me. He had to be or I would never have survived. Never. I'm just hoping that it's all over now. Is that asking too much?"

Watch It!

Use the following space to take notes as you view the video in which Lee Strobel interviews Julia Sweeney—Catholic-turned-atheist; actress, writer, and producer of a one-woman show called "Letting Go of God"; and a veteran of *Saturday Night Live* (known best for her role as the androgynous character Pat)—and Craig Detweiler, a graduate of both the USC Film School and Fuller Seminary. He's also the author of *Matrix of Meanings: Finding God in Pop Culture*.

Discuss It!

1 If God is so good and so powerful, why do you think he allows so much pain and suffering in this world?

2 Some atheists believe that the mere existence of pain and suffering in our world strongly suggests that there really is no God. Do you agree? Why or why not?

> "Either God wants to abolish evil, and cannot; or he can, but does not want to; or he cannot and does not want to. If he wants to, but cannot, he is impotent. If he can, but does not want to, he is wicked. But, if God both can and wants to abolish evil, then how comes evil in the world?"
>
> **Epicurus, 350 BC**

3 In what ways can you relate to the following words written by the Old Testament prophet Habakkuk? Share a personal experience you have had with pain or suffering that caused you to doubt the *existence* or the *goodness* of God.

How long, LORD, must I call for help, but you do not listen? Or cry out to you, "Violence!" but you do not save? Why do you make me look at injustice? Why do you tolerate wrongdoing? Destruction and violence are before me; there is strife, and conflict abounds.... Your eyes are too pure to look on evil; you cannot tolerate wrongdoing. Why then do you tolerate the treach-

erous? Why are you silent while the wicked swallow up those more righteous than themselves? (Habakkuk 1:2–3, 13)

4 At one point Sweeney believed that God put us here on the earth but did not involve himself with us very much. To what extent do you believe God is involved in our lives here on earth? Give reasons for your response.

> "God whispers to us in our pleasures, speaks to us in our conscience, but shouts to us in our pains. Suffering is God's megaphone to rouse a deaf world."
>
> **C. S. Lewis**

5 Craig Detweiler claims pain and suffering are tests of character. How do you respond to this claim? What is the point of pain? Does pain exist for a reason? Are there any possible benefits from pain and suffering?

"Babies are born with multiple birth defects. Genetic disor-
ders plague many of us. An earthquake levels a city, and
thousands lose their lives in the rubble. The Bible teaches
that there is not always a one-to-one correspondence between sin and suffering. When we human beings told God
to shove off, he partially honored our request. Nature began to revolt. The earth was cursed. Genetic breakdown
and disease began. Pain and death became a part of the
human experience. The good creation was marred. We live
in an unjust world. We are born into a world made chaotic
and unfair by a humanity in revolt against its Creator."

Cliffe Knechtle, *Give Me an Answer*

6 In what ways do pain and suffering push you away from God? In what ways do pain and suffering have the capacity to draw you closer to God?

"The LORD is close to the brokenhearted and saves those
who are crushed in spirit."

Psalm 34:18

7 If God has the power to end human suffering right now, why doesn't he do it?

"Believing God is the sovereign creator and in control of the world doesn't mean He is directly, causally connected with everything that happens on this earth. He doesn't make the decision to reach down and shake loose a rock to start every avalanche. When some people hear this kind of thinking, they get nervous. They think I'm limiting God. I'm not. But I am saying God doesn't ordinarily interfere with the natural course of the universe any more often than He directly interferes with man's choices."

Jay Kesler, *Making Life Make Sense*

8 Lee Strobel suggests that it's impossible to create a world with free will and not allow the possibility of pain and suffering. In other words, God cannot create human beings with a total ability to freely make meaningful choices and at the same time control them so they always make good choices. Do you agree with this logic? Why or why not?

9 Do you consider your freedom to choose to be a good gift from God? Why or why not? What would human relationships be like without free will?

"So how do theists respond to arguments like this? They say there is a reason for evil, but it is a mystery. Well, let me tell you this: I'm actually one hundred feet tall even though I only appear to be six feet tall. You ask me for proof of this. I have a simple answer: it's a mystery. Just accept my word for it on faith. And that's just the logic theists use in their discussions of evil."

Atheist Quentin Smith

10 If you could eliminate all evil, suffering, and sin (wrongdoing) in your life by giving up your free will, would you do it? Explain.

11 If there were no sin or wrongdoing in the world, do you think there would be any suffering and evil? Why or why not?

"For whatever reason God chose to make man as he is—limited and suffering and subject to sorrows and death—he had the honesty and courage to take his own medicine. Whatever game he is playing with his creation, he has kept his own rules and played fair. He can exact nothing from man that he has not exacted from himself. He has himself gone through the whole of human experience, from the trivial irritations of family life and the cramping restrictions of hard work and lack of money, to the worst horrors of pain and humiliation, defeat, and death. When he was a man, he played the man. He was born in poverty and he died in disgrace and thought it well worthwhile."

Dorothy Sayers

12 Do you believe in an afterlife free of pain and suffering? Why or why not?

13 Revelation 21:4 says, "He will wipe every tear from their eyes. There will be no more death or mourning or crying or pain, for the old order of things has passed away." Does it bring you any comfort to know that in the afterlife God will put an end to all pain and suffering and evil? Why or why not?

Watch It! Lee's Perspective

I remember interviewing Peter Kreeft, a Catholic philosopher at Boston College, about pain and suffering for my book *The Case for Faith*. "There's no question that the existence of evil is one argument against God," he told me. "But in one of my books I summarize twenty arguments that point persuasively in the other direction, in favor of the existence of God. Atheists must answer all twenty arguments; theists must only answer one."

I agree that the evidence of science and history build a powerful case for God's existence. At the same time, I can understand when people undergo emotional or physical pain and begin to question whether God is really there for them.

Personally, I believe the classic Christian response to pain and suffering makes sense. The only way God could allow us to experience love, the greatest value in the universe, is if he gave us free will so we could choose whether or not to love him and others. Love *must* involve choice. Unfortunately, we've abused our freedom of choice by hurting each other, and that's where most of the world's suffering has come from.

Christian theology also provides an answer for the natural disasters that cause so much harm. As Cliffe Knechtle put it: "When we human beings told God to shove off, he partially honored our request." The result: creation was marred. We no longer live in the world as it was originally designed.

All of this, though, is an intellectual response. Yet Christianity offers so much more, because God himself set aside his exemption from pain and entered into human history, where he endured humiliation, rejection, torture, and death. "Our sufferings become more manageable in light of this," said British pastor John Stott. "There is still a question mark against human suffering, but over it we boldly stamp another mark, the cross which symbolizes divine suffering."

For Stott—and for me—belief in God would be repugnant if it weren't for the cross. "In the real world of pain," Stott said, "how could one worship a God who was immune to it?"

Chart It!

At this point in your spiritual journey, what do you believe about the problem of pain and suffering? On a 1–10 scale, place an X near the spot and phrase that best describes you. Share your selection with the rest of the group and give reasons for placing your X where you did.

1	2	3	4	5	6	7	8	9	10

I'm convinced that God is ultimately responsible for pain and suffering.	I'm unsure why God would allow pain and suffering.	I'm convinced that pain and suffering is the result of mankind's rejection of God.

Study It!

Take some time later this week to check out what the Bible teaches about the problem of pain and suffering.

- Job 5:7
- Job 13:15
- Isaiah 43:2
- John 9:1–41
- John 16:33
- Romans 5:1–21
- Romans 8:12–30
- 2 Corinthians 4:16–18
- Ephesians 6:10–20
- James 1:2–18

THE MYSTERY
OF THE TRINITY?

Read It!

Three in One?

Mrs. Lundquist held a hard-boiled egg in front of her sixth-grade Sunday school class. "So, what is this?" she asked.

"Silly Putty!" Dan shouted. Most of the girls giggled. Doug punched him and muttered, "Shut up."

Kate whispered to Doug, "Jesus wouldn't want you to say 'shut up.'"

"Class," Mrs. Lundquist continued, "somebody please tell me what I'm holding up. Maybe somebody ate one of these this morning before coming to church?"

"We had Pop-Tarts," Caroline responded. "But that's an egg."

Mrs. Lundquist smiled. "Yes, thank you, Caroline. It's an egg, and this egg is going to demonstrate an important aspect of God: the Trinity."

"That's the Father, Son, and Holy Spirit," Caroline stated proudly.

"You're right, Caroline," Mrs. Lundquist affirmed. "The Trinity is a word we use to explain a truth about God: that he exists as three persons in one being. Three distinct persons, but only one God."

"That doesn't make sense," Doug interjected.

"Well, that's why I brought this egg to class this morning," Mrs. Lundquist said. "With the help of this egg and a little imagination, I'd like to try to explain to you the concept of the Trinity. You see, an egg is one thing, right?" The kids nodded, all except Doug, who stared with his head tilted to one side, watching, thinking. "This part I'm tapping, what is it called?"

"The shell," several kids responded.

"Exactly. Is the shell by itself an egg?"

"No," the class said in unison, with Doug still pondering silently.

"Okay, now I'm going to crack it open. See this part? It's called something ..."

"The white!"

"Exactly. Is the white of the egg the whole egg?"

"No!" They were on a roll now.

"Okay, now inside the white there's yet another part to this egg. What's the yellow part called?"

"The yolk!"

"Right! Is the yolk the egg?"

"No!"

"So to have an egg—one complete egg—we need all of these parts together. Three parts, all distinct with special qualities of their own, but united as one. This is an illustration of what God is like, you see." She began pointing to the parts of the egg. "God the Father, God the Son, God the Holy Spirit." She pulled out another egg. "Together," she concluded, holding the unbroken egg high in the air, "they are one."

Some of the kids nodded solemnly, as if they captured the complexity of the Trinity in that instant. Some restlessly watched the clock. Doug, however, still stared at the egg. "That doesn't explain it," he answered. "That doesn't explain anything."

"What?" Mrs. Lundquist looked toward him, slightly flustered, bringing the unbroken egg down, almost cradling it. "You say you don't understand it?"

"It just doesn't make sense to me," Doug answered. "You have to add up all three parts of the egg to make it an egg, but you don't add up the Father, Son, and Holy Spirit to make God. Aren't they all supposed to be God themselves?"

Mrs. Lundquist was taken aback. *Hmmmm*, she thought to herself, *he's right—the egg analogy is a bit, well ... scrambled.* She looked at the clock. There wasn't much time to spare.

"Okay, Doug, you've got a point there," she said. Doug smiled—a little too broadly, she thought to herself. "Let's try another approach. I know you've been a good student in school, so you probably know a few things about science." Doug nodded confidently. "Well," she continued, "you might remember something about the qualities of H_2O, then."

Caroline held up her hand. "H_2O is water."

"That's right, Caroline," Mrs. Lundquist continued, but she was zeroing in on Doug. "Water is the liquid form of H_2O, but what other forms can it take?"

"Ice!" said Kate.

"Yes, ice, frozen water, a solid. What else?"

"Steam," Doug said.

"That's right," Mrs. Lundquist nodded. "H_2O can also be in the form of steam or vapor. Is water vapor H_2O?"

"Yes," Doug said.

"Is ice still H_2O?" she asked.

"Yes," Doug answered.

"And what about liquid water?"

"Yes, that's still H_2O," he stated.

"Do you understand it, then, Doug? Three forms or expressions, each distinct and individual, but each equally H_2O. Do you see how that can help explain God in three persons—God the Father, God the Son, and God the Holy Spirit—yet as one being?"

The class was quiet except for the soft scrape of someone's shoe against the leg of a chair. Sunday school classes throughout the building would all be dismissed in seconds. "What do you think, Doug?" Mrs. Lundquist pressed. "Does that help explain the Trinity to you?"

Doug furrowed his brow. "Well, not exactly," he said slowly as he continued to think about the analogy. "H_2O can't be liquid, water, and gas at the same time. So are you saying that God takes on different forms as the Father, Son, and Holy Spirit at different times? Now he's the Father, then—*poof!* Now he's the Son?"

Mrs. Lundquist's eyes got wide. "Oh, no, I'm not saying that," she said. "All three persons of the Trinity exist simultaneously—that means at the same time. God doesn't morph from one form to the other."

"Then I don't think H_2O is a very good illustration either," Doug concluded. "In fact, what if there is no such thing as three forms of God in one?" He paused when Kate gasped. "Or," he continued, "maybe it just wasn't supposed to be explained in the first place. Maybe God wants to be harder to understand than an egg yolk, or an ice cube. Maybe he wants to stay a mystery."

The bell rang, and the classroom emptied before Mrs. Lundquist could say, "Have a good week." *Maybe*, she mused as she leaned against the wall, *the Trinity is a mystery after all.*

Watch It!

Use the following space to take notes as you view the video in which Lee Strobel interviews Rabbi Tovia Singer, a radio host on Israel National Radio and author of the book *Let's Get Biblical*, and Dr. William Lane Craig, a research professor of philosophy at the Talbot School of Theology and author of numerous books, including *Reasonable Faith* and *Philosophical Foundations for a Christian Worldview.*

Discuss It!

1 What do you believe about God? Is there one God, no God, many gods, or one God in three persons? How is your *current* belief about God similar or dissimilar to what you believed when you were growing up?

2 How would you define the Trinity? In your definition, are the Father, Son and Holy Spirit equals or is there a hierarchy? Are the Father, Son, and Holy Spirit three *different* gods or three persons of the *same* God all wrapped up in one? What are the respective roles of the Father, Son, and Holy Spirit?

"The word 'Trinity,' first used in its Greek form *trias* by Theophilus of Antioch (circa AD 180), is not found in Scripture, but the conception is there both implicitly and explicitly."
F. L. Cross

3 William Craig explains that God the Father, God the Son, and God the Holy Spirit are three distinct persons, but all equally God with three different roles. In what ways does this explanation make sense to you and in what ways does it not make sense?

4 What do the following verses from the Old and New Testaments teach about the nature of God and Jesus Christ? On what points do they agree or disagree?

Old Testament

"I am the first and I am the last; apart from me there is no God.... You are my witnesses. Is there any God besides me? No, there is no other Rock; I know not one." (Isaiah 44:6b, 8b)

"I am the LORD, and there is no other; apart from me there is no God. I will strengthen you, though you have not acknowledged me, so that from the rising of the sun to the place of its setting people may know there is none besides me. I am the LORD, and there is no other." (Isaiah 45:5–6)

"Turn to me and be saved, all you ends of the earth; for I am God, and there is no other." (Isaiah 45:22)

For to us a child is born, to us a son is given, and the government will be on his shoulders. And he will be called Wonderful Counselor, Mighty God, Everlasting Father, Prince of Peace. (Isaiah 9:6)

He was despised and rejected by mankind, a man of suffering, and familiar with pain. Like one from whom people hide their faces he was despised, and we held him in low esteem. Surely he took up our pain and bore our suffering, yet we considered him punished by God, stricken by him, and afflicted. But he was pierced for our transgressions, he was crushed for our iniquities; the punishment that brought us peace was on him, and by his wounds we are healed. (Isaiah 53:3–5)

Then Isaiah said, "Hear now, you house of David! Is it not enough to try the patience of humans? Will you try the patience of my God also? Therefore the Lord himself will give you a sign: The virgin will conceive and give birth to a son, and will call him Immanuel." (Isaiah 7:13–14)

Hear, O Israel: The LORD our God, the LORD is one. (Deuteronomy 6:4)

New Testament

There is one body and one Spirit, just as you were called to one hope when you were called; one Lord, one faith, one baptism; one God and Father of all, who is over all and through all and in all. (Ephesians 4:4–6)

[Jesus answered,] "I and the Father are one." ... "We are not stoning you for any good work," [his Jewish opponents] replied, "but for blasphemy, because you, a mere man, claim to be God." (John 10:30, 33)

"The most important one," answered Jesus, "is this: 'Hear, O Israel, the Lord our God, the Lord is one.'"..."Well said, teacher," the man replied. "You are right in saying that God is one and there is no other but him." (Mark 12:29, 32)

Thomas said to [Jesus], "My Lord and my God." (John 20:28)

> "Therefore go and make disciples of all nations, baptizing them in the name of the Father and of the Son and of the Holy Spirit."
>
> **Matthew 28:19**

5 Dr. Craig claims that the Old and the New Testaments are equally inspired by God, while Rabbi Singer contends that only the Old Testament is inspired by God. What do you think? Explain your response.

6 Lee Strobel points out that there are four clear teachings in the New Testament: (1) the Father is God, (2) the Son, Jesus, is God, (3) the Holy Spirit is God, and (4) there is only one God. If it could be substantiated that the Bible does in fact make these four claims, to what extent would that be sufficient evidence to conclude that God is triune? Why or why not?

> "God the Father is fully God. God the Son is fully God. God the Holy Spirit is fully God. The Bible presents this as fact. It does not explain it."
>
> **Billy Graham**

7 Rabbi Singer believes that the Holy Spirit is the dynamic presence of God but not a separate person. What do you believe about the Holy Spirit? According to the following verses from the Old and New Testaments, what does the Bible teach about the Holy Spirit?

Old Testament

Now the earth was formless and empty, darkness was over the surface of the deep, and the Spirit of God was hovering over the waters. (Genesis 1:2)

The Spirit of God has made me; the breath of the Almighty gives me life. (Job 33:4)

But it is the spirit in a person, the breath of the Almighty, that gives them understanding. (Job 32:8)

If it were his intention and he withdrew his spirit and breath, all humanity would perish together and mankind would return to the dust. (Job 34:14–15)

New Testament

Now the Lord is the Spirit, and where the Spirit of the Lord is, there is freedom. (2 Corinthians 3:17)

Because you are his sons, God sent the Spirit of his Son into our hearts, the Spirit who calls out, "Abba, Father." (Galatians 4:6)

But when he, the Spirit of truth, comes, he will guide you into all the truth. (John 16:13a)

8 Rabbi Singer contends that Jesus isn't the Son of God, which Dr. Craig refutes. What do you think? Is Jesus the Son of God or not? Give reasons for your response.

> "By saying God has one essence and three persons it is meant that he has one 'What' and three 'Whos.' The three Whos (persons) each share the same What (essence). So God is a unity of essence with a plurality of persons. Each person is different, yet they share a common nature."
>
> **Norman Geisler, PhD**

9 What reasons can you give that support the idea that Jesus was God? What reasons can you give that support the idea that Jesus was not God?

10 Dr. Craig points out that one of the most rapidly growing segments of Judaism is Messianic Judaism, fully Jewish people who decide to place their belief and trust in Jesus as Messiah. These are strict monotheistic Jews who have become convinced that Jesus is the God who fulfills their Hebrew faith. Why do you suppose these people are changing their minds about the nature of Jesus and God?

Watch It! Lee's Perspective

There's no question about it—the Trinity is not an easy concept to grasp. Perhaps it's no mistake that while the Bible freely uses various metaphors to illuminate its theology, nowhere does it offer an illustration to describe the Trinity. Indeed, it's a concept so sophisticated that it defies simple analogies.

Theologian Paul Enns doesn't even particularly like the word itself, because it stresses the three persons and not the unity within the Trinity. He prefers a German word that means "three-oneness." Still another descriptive word is "Triunity." In fact, the difficulty of coming up with an appropriate label is just one more illustration of how complicated God's nature really is.

Frankly, that shouldn't surprise us. The God who created the universe and who sustains it day by day is bound to be far beyond our mortal ability to fully understand. To me, the key remains this: does the Bible clearly communicate that the Father is God, that Jesus is God, and that the Holy Spirit is God? And does it emphatically declare that there is one God?

The answer to both those questions is yes. We can wrestle with trying to comprehend the Trinity, but if the Bible is accurate, then we can't ignore the fact that the Trinity is true. And contrary to some claims, it's not a contradiction.

Says theologian Norman Geisler: "The Trinity is not the belief that God is three persons and only one person at the same time and in the same sense. That would be a contradiction. Rather, it is the belief that there are three persons in one *nature*. This may be a mystery, but it is not a contradiction. That is, it may go beyond reason's ability to comprehend completely, but it does not go against reason's ability to apprehend consistently."

Chart It!

At this point in your spiritual journey, what do you believe about the Trinity? On a 1–10 scale, place an X near the spot and phrase that best describes you. Share your selection with the rest of the group and give reasons for placing your X where you did.

1	2	3	4	5	6	7	8	9	10

I'm not convinced that God the Father, God the Son, and God the Holy Spirit are three distinct persons, all equally God with three different roles.

I'm unsure what I believe about the Trinity.

I'm convinced that God the Father, God the Son, and God the Holy Spirit are three distinct persons, all equally God with three different roles.

Study It!

Take some time later this week to check out what the Bible teaches about the Trinity.

- Isaiah 9:1–8
- Isaiah 43:10–13
- Isaiah 45:4–6, 18, 22
- Isaiah 52:13–53:12
- John 1
- John 10
- John 20:24–31
- Ephesians 1:11–14
- 1 Timothy 2:5

DO CHRISTIANS AND MUSLIMS WORSHIP THE SAME GOD?

Read It!

No Difference?

David carefully compared the rows and rows of bottled water. It was hard to read the small print on the labels, but as far as he could tell, all the brands looked pretty much the same.

"Seems like they're identical," he concluded aloud as he tossed a case into his cart, "except for price. And I'll bet the lower priced ones actually taste better. Besides, for all I know, they're all probably made at the same plant using different labels."

"Yes, it's true, they do that," whispered an elderly women standing nearby, clutching a wad of coupons in her left hand. "I always buy generic whenever I can. There's really no difference."

On his way home, he stopped by the drugstore to pick up some cold medicine his wife needed. He had some extra time to ask the pharmacist for some expert advice about which brand to go with. "It really doesn't matter, sir. If you read the ingredients you'll see that they're all basically the same." David was surprised to hear the pharmacist's explanation and grabbed the brand they'd always used before.

Back in his car, David heard a radio advertisement for a mortgage refinancing deal. *Wow, those rates are low,* he thought, *I'd better hurry up and call before I miss out on a chance for a sweet deal to lower our monthly payments.* As he jotted down the phone number, he had second thoughts. *Then again, why bother? I might as well stick with the mortgage company I have now—I'm sure they'll be able to get me the same mortgage rates advertised here.*

When David was finally home, a colleague from work called. "What do you think about the buyout they announced today?"

"I doubt if things will be that different," David replied. "In the end, the new corporation will want us to do the same things we've always been doing. That's why they bought us—they know we're good at what we do. After they change the logo on the letterhead, our lives will be about the same as they've always been. We'll show up at meetings and hit our usual quotas and deadlines as best we can."

After dinner, David turned on the news channel. In a special religion segment, the reporter compared some of the beliefs and practices of various world religions. Christianity, Judaism, Islam, Buddhism, and Hinduism were each highlighted. Representatives from each of those religions were interviewed at length, and asked similar questions about their understanding of God, the afterlife, and truth sources. The segment showed various scenes of the faithful from each religion assembling at services, each in their own way.

David's wife turned to him. "I don't know why the reporter is only focusing on their differences," she said. "Why not concentrate on their similarities? After all, aren't they all worshiping the same God?"

David paused for a moment as the reporter gave her concluding remarks. "I don't know," he said, "but it seems like everywhere you turn, things appear to be different at first, but in the end, they're pretty much the same."

A shampoo commercial came on during the break. "Yes, I'll bet you're right," he added, "I'll bet they're all worshiping the same God after all."

Watch It!

Use the following space to take notes as you view the video in which Lee Strobel interviews Deborah Caldwell, a Christian and senior religion producer at the multi-faith website beliefnet .com; Hesham A. Hassaballa, a physician, Muslim columnist for beliefnet.com, and author of the forthcoming book *The Beliefnet Guide to Islam*; and Ergun Caner who was raised as a Muslim but converted to Christianity in 1982. He currently teaches church history at Liberty University and wrote the award-winning book *Unveiling Islam* as well as *Christian Jihad*, which provides a provocative look at the Christian crusades.

Discuss It!

1 How do you feel about the fact that people believe so differently—and strongly—when it comes to religion? What reasons can you give for these differences?

2 Do you think it's important to keep an open dialogue going with people from different religious beliefs and backgrounds, or is it better to avoid these conversations altogether? What are the advantages and disadvantages of such a practice?

"There is no one alive today who knows enough to say with confidence whether one religion has been greater than all others."

Arnold Toynbee

3 Deborah Caldwell expresses concern that the process of emphasizing religious differences causes unnecessary separation and division in our society. Do you agree? Why or why not? Do we all have to believe the same thing to get along?

4 What is your definition of *religious tolerance*? Does it mean that we should strive to identify ways religions are the same? Does it mean that we should never discuss religious differences? Does it mean that we should never hold to a belief system that excludes another belief system? Is *religious tolerance* a positive or negative term? Explain.

> "It was more than I could believe that Jesus was the only incarnate Son of God. And that only he who believed in him would have everlasting life. If God could have sons, all of us were his sons. If Jesus was like God ... then all men were like God and could be God himself."
>
> **Mohandas K. Gandhi**

5 What's the difference between freedom *of* religion and freedom *from* religion? Which do you think should be the goal of a free society? Explain.

6 Explain the connection among the following:

- Build bridges of religious commonality.
- Clearly define religious differences and similarities.
- Openly discuss and acknowledge religious differences and similarities.
- Seek to understand one another.

7 Ergun Caner states that he is willing to fight for the freedom to believe whatever people choose to believe, but he is unwilling to let people redefine the God of the Bible into something inaccurate. Is this a reasonable expectation? Why or why not?

8 Hesham Hassaballa believes that the message from all the prophets throughout the ages was the same. Do you agree? Why or why not?

9 Do you think the Jews and Christians worship the same God? Why or why not?

> "Jesus was only a messenger of Allah.... Far is it removed from His transcendent majesty that [Allah] should have a son."
>
> **The Koran, Surah 4:171**

10 Consider the following list of core beliefs of Islam and Christianity. What are some significant similarities or differences between the two faiths?

Islam	Christianity
Allah is the one true God; there is no Trinity (Father, Son, and Holy Spirit).	God is triune: one God in three persons (Father, Son, and Holy Spirit).
Allah is hidden and distant from humanity.	Christians worship and pursue a personal and loving relationship with God through Jesus Christ.
Jesus is one of many prophets of which Muhammad is superior. Jesus is Messiah, but not divine.	Jesus is God incarnate.
The Bible is inspired, but flawed; the Koran is superior to all other holy books.	The Bible, consisting of the Old and New Testaments, is the only divinely inspired, infallible source of truth.
The Koran teaches that Jesus never claimed to be God.	The Bible teaches that Jesus not only claimed to be God, but he proved it by dying on the cross and rising from the dead.
Abraham is the forefather of the faith through whom all the world will be blessed.	Abraham is the forefather of the faith through whom all the world will be blessed.

Islam	Christianity
The soul is eternal and there will be a judgment day with a heaven and hell to follow.	The soul is eternal and there will be a judgment day with a heaven and hell to follow.
Jesus did not die for sin.	Jesus' death is the only payment for human sin; we must each individually accept this free gift to be saved.
Entrance into heaven is based on one's performance on earth and adherence to the five pillars of Islam.	Entrance into heaven is not based on performance but solely dependent on one's earthly relationship with Jesus Christ.

11 Do you think Muslims and Christians actually worship the same God, even though they may view or understand him differently? Explain.

12 Hassaballa believes Christians and Muslims worship the same God. Caner argues that the Muslim God is different from the Christian God because Muslims deny the deity of Jesus. Do you agree that this is a significant difference? Why or why not?

> "I am the way and the truth and the life. No one comes to the Father except through me."
>
> **Jesus Christ, John 14:6**

13 Hassaballa believes that Jesus was the Messiah but not the God-man. What's erroneous, if anything, about this belief? How is it possible for Jesus to be the Messiah without being the God-man? Do you agree with Caner that if Jesus was not God, his life and death were meaningless? Explain.

14 What is the basis for your beliefs, if any, about God? What would be sufficient to cause you to reconsider your beliefs and accept another faith?

Watch It! Lee's Perspective

I have a Muslim friend. We often grill steaks in my backyard and talk about faith. I tell him about the historical evidence that convinces me Christianity is true; he tells me why he disagrees and why he's an adherent of Islam. Sure, the discussion gets heated at times, but we don't pull out knives, attack each other, or belittle each other's beliefs. Through it all, we've remained friends.

Do we worship the same God? No, we don't. Take a look at the list of differences between Islam and Christianity included as part of this session. There are irreconcilable differences between the two. God cannot be triune and not triune at the same time. Jesus cannot be God's Son and a mortal messenger at the same time. God cannot be the intimate Father of Christianity and the distant and detached deity of Islam at the same time. Salvation cannot be solely through grace and be merited by good works at the same time.

However, I can be a Christian and still love my Muslim friend, as I trust he can remain my friend despite our differences. It would be wrong for us to paper over the distinctives of our faiths and pretend they say the same thing when they clearly don't. But it would be wrong, too, if we let our differences drive us to hatred or violence toward each other.

Truth should never be sacrificed on a false altar of religious tolerance. We can be civilized toward each other and still disagree, but my friend and I simply cannot be right at the same time. The laws of logic say it's impossible.

For me, the question is always this: where does the evidence point? Does it — or does it not — support the claim of Jesus that he's the sole pathway to God? My goal is to encourage everyone to make an informed decision about that topic.

So let me ask you: where do you stand right now on this paramount issue — and why?

Chart It!

At this point in your spiritual journey, what do you believe about the differences or similarities between Islam and Christianity? On a 1–10 scale, place an X near the spot and phrase that best describes you. Share your selection with the rest of the group and give reasons for placing your X where you did.

1	2	3	4	5	6	7	8	9	10

I'm convinced that Muslims and Christians worship the same God.	I'm unsure about whether Muslims and Christians worship the same God.	I'm convinced that Muslims and Christians do not worship the same God.

Study It!

Take some time in the coming days to check out what the Bible teaches about the identity of God.

- Matthew 5:17–20
- Matthew 10:24–39
- John 3:16
- John 14:6–7
- Acts 4:12
- Hebrews 12:2
- 1 John 3:4–5
- 1 John 4:1–10